TO THE STUDENT

Take It Easy is a book about idioms. In fact, *take it easy* is an idiom—a group of words combined to express an idea beyond the meaning of the individual words. For example, the word *take* often means "to get into one's hands" or "to receive." The word *easy* generally means "not difficult." However, when these words are combined, as in *take it easy*, they form a unit that means "relax" or "make oneself free from care."

Many of the verbs used in English idioms are from Old English (Anglo-Saxon) or Middle English, ancestors of the English we use today. Their one-word equivalents, on the other hand, are frequently based on Latin words. For example:

Old English		**Latin**
have over	=	*invite* (to one's home)
put on	=	*deceive* (for fun)

In informal settings, native speakers often use idioms rather than their Latin equivalents. For example:

I'd like to *have* you *over*. (less formal)
I'd like to *invite* you to my home. (more formal)
I think you're *putting* me *on*. (less formal)
I think you're *deceiving* me for fun. (more formal)

This does not mean that all idioms are so informal as to be considered slang or incorrect English. Most are acceptable forms of expression and are found in speeches as well as movies, novels as well as newspapers. In this book, idioms limited to informal conversation are marked "informal" in Review the Idioms at the end of each chapter.

Take It Easy will help you *notice*, *understand*, and *use* 166 verb idioms. By teaching you idioms, it will help you communicate like a native speaker of English. While introducing you to the everyday language of the United States, the book will also expand your understanding of the culture of the country. You will read about differences in conversational styles between men and women, the origin of blue jeans, the richest man in the world, a best-selling novel, and popular movies. You will also discuss contemporary issues, such as homelessness, consumerism, and immigration policy. This approach makes the study of idioms informative as well as enjoyable.

Take It Easy is designed for use in class, but it may also be used for self-study because the answers to many exercises are provided in the back of the book. Whether you study alone or with other students, learning a language can be challenging. The best approach is to practice all you can, not worry about mistakes, and *take it easy*!

To the Teacher

Take It Easy is designed to help English-as-a-second-language learners *notice, understand,* and *use* 166 verb idioms. The expression *take it easy* is one of the high-frequency idioms presented in this text.

The readings and exercises in *Take It Easy* are geared to high-intermediate to advanced ESL students. It is at these levels that students begin to notice these complex expressions. By the high-intermediate level, students have achieved a degree of fluency that lets them start to experiment with idioms in their own speech and writing.

Most of the idioms in *Take It Easy* are phrasal verbs (verb + particle), such as *hold on, branch out, cut [it] out,* and *wrap [it] up.* The book also presents some prepositional verbs (verb + preposition), such as *head for* and *cope with.* In addition to the two-word combinations mentioned above, the book offers phrasal-prepositional combinations (verb + particle + preposition), such as *get away with (it)* and *talk [it] over with (them).* Finally, a few idioms are included that do not contain particles or prepositions, such as *take it easy, make money,* and *surf the Net.*

Each of the ten chapters focuses on a subject or theme, such as conversational styles, love, anger, or driving and directions. A warm-up activity helps students explore the chapter's theme before the idioms are introduced. Next, from fifteen to eighteen idioms related to the theme are incorporated in a meaningful context, ranging from a conversation to a corporate profile, that is, from informal English to more formal English. Follow-up exercises and activities help learners become aware of the idioms, begin to understand the meaning of the idioms, and develop confidence in producing these expressions. In the exercises and activities, students figure out the meaning of each idiom based on the introductory context, then work on comprehension of the idioms in new contexts, such as greeting cards, snippets of conversation, and excerpts from authentic articles in newspapers. Listening activities (based on conversations, commercials, radio reports, lectures, interviews, and movie reviews) provide additional contexts in which students get exposure to the idioms. Speaking exercises (such as sharing personal information, participating in role plays, reacting to a poem, or giving advice) offer students a chance to use the idioms in their own speech. In writing exercises, students use the idioms from the chapter when they paraphrase reports, respond to pictures, and compose stories that go with headlines.

This new edition of *Take It Easy* offers a number of improvements over the original edition. In particular, it includes cultural information and statistics on life in the United States. It provides exercises that help the learner figure out the meaning of each idiom presented in the introductory reading. It also includes more listening activities with a variety of real-life contexts. As students move from noticing and understanding idioms (in reading and listening) to using them (in speaking and writing), they are given opportunities to talk about themselves and give advice to others in idiomatic English. This edition also offers games to challenge learners and liven up the classroom. Finally, a new review section appears after each five chapters. (Each chapter is self-contained, but a class would need to complete all five chapters to take advantage of each review.)

Second Edition

Take It Easy

AMERICAN IDIOMS

Pamela McPartland-Fairman

GLOBAL VILLAGE TORONTO
(The Language Workshop)
180 Bloor Street West, Suite 202
Toronto, Ontario
M5S 2V6 Canada

Longman

Take It Easy: American Idioms, Second Edition

Pearson Education, 10 Bank Street, White Plains, NY 10606

Editorial director: Allen Ascher
Executive editor: Louisa Hellegers
Acquisitions editor: Laura Le Dréan
Development manager: Penny LaPorte
Development editor: Lise Minovitz
Director of design and production: Rhea Banker
Associate director of electronic production: Aliza Greenblatt
Managing editor: Linda Moser
Production manager: Ray Keating
Production editor: Noël Vreeland Carter
Electronic production editor: Wendy Wolf
Senior manufacturing manager: Patrice Fraccio
Manufacturing supervisor: Edith Pullman
Photo research: Marianne Carello
Cover design: Carey Davies
Text design: Curt Belshe
Text art: Andrew Lange, Catherine Doyle Sullivan, Wendy Wolf
Text credits: See pp. 199–200.

Library of Congress Cataloging-in-Publication Data

McPartland-Fairman, Pamela.
  Take it easy: American idioms/Pamela McPartland-Fairman–2nd ed.
    p. cm
  ISBN: 0-13-660812-4
  1. English language—Textbooks for foreign speakers. 2. English language—United
States—Idioms—Problems, exercises, etc. 3. Americanisms—Problems, exercises, etc.
I. Title: American idioms. II. Title.

PE1128 .M327 2000
428.2'4—dc21

                                                                    99-056986

1 2 3 4 5 6 7 8 9 10—CRK—05 04 03 02 01 00

CONTENTS

- be at a loss for words • be driving at • bring up • come on • cut off
- get along • go ahead • hold on • lighten up • put on • spell out
- start over • take it easy • talk into • talk over • throw off • wrap up

- be on the market • bet on • bow out • branch out • build up • buy out
- cash in on • change course • do business with • make money • make up
- pay off • put out • set up • ship out • surf the Net • take off • work out

- clean out • coop up • eat in • eat out • fix up • get around • have over
- hold onto • keep up • look out on • make room for • move in • move out
- pass up • stay up • take one's pick

- be behind bars • be on the run • break in • do time • get away with
- get out of hand • go to trial • gun down • hide out in • lock up • make off with
- own up to • pick up • put the blame on • tie up • track down

- be fond of • be crazy about • bowl over • come across as • do in • drive crazy
- fall for • fall in love • fool around • hold one's own with • keep a stiff upper lip
- keep an eye on • run into • shift gears • turn out

In the new edition, more phrasal verbs are presented. The book also contains more expressions that are highly idiomatic (for example, *pull up, wind up, come up with*), and fewer expressions that are transparent in meaning (for example, *calm down, slow down, start out*).

As in the first edition, many idioms here were chosen because of their frequency of use in everyday life. This "use" represents not only daily conversations, but also television news reports, articles in newspapers such as *The New York Times* and in magazines such as *Newsweek* and *People*. While certain idioms are labeled "informal" (for example, *come on, lighten up,* and *take it easy*), there is no slang in this book because slang tends to become outdated quickly.

This new edition of *Take It Easy*, like the first edition, helps learners discover for themselves the position of pronoun objects in phrasal verbs vs. prepositional verbs, *pull [it] over* vs. *pull into (it)*. In this second edition, however, the position of the pronominal object of phrasal verbs is marked by a bracket: [ ], while the position of the object of the preposition in prepositional verbs is indicated by a parentheses: ( ). With this innovation, learners can see at a glance if an idiom is a phrasal verb or a prepositional verb. This important information appears in Review the Idioms, which is now conveniently located at the end of each chapter. Grammatical restrictions and levels of formality (register) are also given in Review the Idioms. Students may wish to refer to this section or write notes there while working through the activities in each chapter.

Almost all of the idioms in *Take It Easy* fall into one of six grammatical patterns. The patterns are not mentioned explicitly in the chapters because of the danger that learners will become so preoccupied with the patterns, little time will be left to grasp the meaning of the idioms and how they are used. Remember: when teaching idioms, *take it easy*!

SIX GRAMMATICAL PATTERNS

While it is not recommended that the patterns be taught, they are offered here for those instructors (and students) who wish to review them. Most of the idioms fall into one of three categories: Phrasal Verbs, Prepositional Verbs, and Phrasal-Prepositional Verbs. Within each category there are transitive verbs (which require an object) and intransitive verbs (which do not require an object). (Note: some verbs can be both transitive and intransitive.) The six patterns are:

A. PHRASAL VERBS

1. intransitive verb + particle   __ __   hold on, move in, eat in, branch out

2. transitive verb + particle   __ [ ] __   have [them] over, keep [it] up, set [it] up

B. PREPOSITIONAL VERBS

3. intransitive verb + preposition   __ __ ( )   cope with (it), fall for (her), bet on (it)

4. transitive verb + preposition   __ [ ] __ ( )   talk [them] into (it)

5. intransitive verb + particle + preposition   __ __ __ ( )   cash in on (it), get away with (it)

6. transitive verb + particle + preposition   __ [ ] __ __ ( )   point [it] out to (them)

Take It Easy also includes idiomatic expressions that contain other parts of speech, including nouns, adjectives, and adverbs. Many of these expressions fit into the same grammatical patterns given above. For example, *ask for (trouble)* fits into number 3 and *keep [an eye] on (it)* fits into number 4.

ACKNOWLEDGMENTS

Twenty years after writing the first edition of *Take It Easy* and receiving many comments and much correspondence from teachers and students, I am very pleased to present this second edition. When the first edition came out, idioms were ignored in ESL texts. Most students reported that they had never heard of phrasal verbs. The only published works were idiom dictionaries. Today, phrasal verbs and other idiomatic combinations have been incorporated in many textbooks in the field, and several books are dedicated exclusively to this aspect of English. I hope that *Take It Easy* has contributed to this change.

Several people have played key roles in this new edition. While still at Prentice Hall Regents, Mary Jane Peluso and Sheryl Olinsky got the revision underway and supervised the review process, with Vivian Garcia collating the reviews. The reviewers, Jonne Smith Lynn Stafford-Yilmaz, Cynthia Wiseman, and Mary Wong, all experienced in the field, made practical suggestions, many of which I was able to add to this edition.

With the creation of Pearson Education from Addison Wesley Longman and Prentice Hall Regents came a new editorial and production staff. I am especially indebted to my development editor for her astute criticism and generous advice with the entire manuscript. Many thanks to Lise Minovitz, Noël Vreeland Carter, and Wendy Wolf for their careful attention to the manuscript while it was in production. Marianne S. Carello cheerfully and conscientiously helped with photo and fact searches. Laura Le Dréan, Acquisitions Editor, tackled each problem with professionalism as well as common sense, and maintained a very enjoyable working relationship from start to finish. Early on, Allen Ascher, Editorial Director, helped me examine how the second edition would differ from, and hopefully improve on, the first. I thank him for that and for many discussions of methods and materials while we were colleagues at the Intensive English Language Institute of Hunter College.

Most of all, I thank my husband, Huck Fairman, for his honest reactions to the introductory readings, and his helpful suggestions for improving them. His constant support and stimulation make the creative process possible.

Pamela McPartland-Fairman

Chapter 1

CONVERSATIONAL STYLES

GETTING STARTED

1. **Discuss the Topic**   In a small group, discuss the following cartoons. What do they say about the differences between men and women? Do you agree? Do these differences between men and women apply in your country? Do they cause problems in relationships?

"She expects me to remember things just because they're important."

(from *The New Yorker*)

"Don't you just love talking up a storm?"[1]

(from *The New Yorker*)

---

[1] *talking up a storm*: talking a lot

INTRODUCTION OF IDIOMS

2. Read Between the Lines   Read the conversation. With a partner, try to understand what it means. Then do Exercise 3.

Do I Have to Spell It Out?

KAREN: Mark, remember last Saturday?

MARK: Last Saturday? (*He places his bookmark in his book.*) **Hold on**.

KAREN: Yes, I asked if you wanted to go dancing with Kathi and Peter.

(*Mark frowns and seems annoyed.*)

MARK: Oh no. You're not **bringing** that **up** again, are you?

KAREN: Whoa, **take it easy**. I'm mentioning it because I was reading in this book how women and men want different things from conversations.

MARK: (*warily*) And?

KAREN: (*looking down to read*) For instance, it says here that in conversations men often try to establish control . . . maintain their independence . . . avoid failure.

(*Mark is not sure he understands or agrees. He seems to **be at a loss for words**.*)

KAREN: Is that true?

MARK: (*shifting in his seat*) No, of course not. When you asked if I wanted to go dancing, I simply said no. That was it.

KAREN: Is it possible you were really trying to maintain your independence by saying no?

MARK: Are you **putting** me **on**? **Come on**, Karen. **Lighten up**.

(*Karen frowns.*)

MARK: I don't understand. I thought we **wrapped up** this particular topic last Saturday. Do we have to **start** all **over** again?

KAREN: You **cut** me **off** is what happened! But this book has helped me understand that you didn't want to be told what to do. Now, do you want to hear what the book says that *women* want from conversations?

MARK: (*sighing*) OK. Why not? **Go ahead**.

KAREN: It says that for women, conversations are opportunities for closeness. Women basically want to **get along with** others. In conversations, women ask for and give support, and try to reach agreement.

(*Mark shakes his head and turns back to his book.*)

MARK: So you just wanted a little support? If that's what you **were driving at**, why didn't you just say so?

KAREN: I thought you'd understand that it was important to me. I didn't think I'd have to **spell** it **out**.

MARK: Why didn't you tell me that you had already **talked** it **over** with Kathi and Peter and that you had decided you wanted to go?

KAREN: I . . . uh . . . was hoping that you would express some interest, since you knew that the three of us liked to dance. I was hoping I wouldn't have to **talk** you **into** it.

MARK: (*frowning*) Well, your question **threw** me **off**. I thought you were really asking me if I *wanted* to.

KAREN: I was hoping that you'd see that *I* wanted to. Yes, I guess I *was* looking for support.

MARK: (*thinking*) Maybe this is all too subtle for a guy.

UNDERSTANDING THE MEANING

3. Line by Line   With a partner, mark the answer that explains the conversation on pages 2–3. Then look at the conversation and find the sentence with the same meaning. Write that sentence below.

1. Mark is reading a book when Karen begins to talk to him. What does he tell her to do?

   a. [ ] Hold the book for him.
   b. [ ] Mark his page in the book.
   c. [×] Wait a minute.

   Sentence:_____

2. Mark gets annoyed when Karen mentions their conversation about going dancing. What does Karen tell Mark to do?

   a. [ ] Discuss it.
   b. [×] Relax.
   c. [ ] Listen.

   Sentence:_____

3. When Karen tells Mark that men try to establish control in conversation, how does he react?

   a. [×] He's speechless.
   b. [ ] He agrees with her.
   c. [×] He feels as if he's losing the argument.

   Sentence:_____

4. Karen asks Mark if he was trying to remain independent by saying no to her invitation to go dancing. What does Mark tell Karen to do?

   a. [ ] Lose weight.
   b. [×] Be less serious.
   c. [ ] Change the color of her hair.

   Sentence:_____

5. How does Mark feel about discussing the topic of dancing now?

   a. [X] He doesn't want to begin again.
   b. [ ] He wants to be the one to begin the conversation.
   c. [ ] He wants to discuss the topic.

   Sentence: _____

6. What does Karen say that Mark did when they first discussed the possibility of going dancing?

   a. [ ] He insulted her.
   b. [X] He interrupted her.
   c. [ ] He cut his hand.

   Sentence: _____

7. According to the book Karen is reading, what is important to women?

   a. [ ] To be able to speak in a conversation
   b. [ ] To end the conversation
   c. [X] To have friendly relationships with others

   Sentence: _____

8. Karen thought Mark would understand that going dancing was important to her. What was she surprised about?

   a. [X] She didn't think it would be necessary to say exactly how important it was.
   b. [ ] She didn't think she would have to put her invitation in writing.
   c. [ ] She didn't think she would have to tell him where they were going dancing first.

   Sentence: _____

9. Karen was hoping that Mark would show some interest in going dancing. What was she hoping she wouldn't have to do?

   a. [ ] Discuss it one more time.
   b. [X] Convince him to go.
   c. [ ] Teach him how to dance.

   Sentence: _____

10. What did Mark say about Karen's question ("Do you want to go dancing with Kathi and Peter?")?

    a. [ ] It made him think.
    b. [X] It gave him the wrong idea about what she really wanted.
    c. [ ] It helped him understand what she really wanted.

    Sentence: _____

4. Paraphrase Mark's Monolog   Read the monolog by Mark below. Work with a partner. For each idiom in bold, find the meaning in the box. Write the letter of the idiom next to its meaning.

Last Saturday, Karen asked me if I wanted to go dancing with her and another couple. I really didn't want to, so I said no. Well, a week later, she (a.) **brought** it **up** again! Then she started telling me about some book she was reading by Deborah Tannen. It said that men try to maintain their independence and avoid failure in conversations. She wanted to know if I was trying to maintain my independence by saying no to her. I couldn't believe it. I said, "Karen, are you (b.) **putting** me **on**? (c.) **Come on!**" As far as I was concerned, we had (d.) **wrapped up** the discussion the week before. But then she wanted to tell me what the book said about women in conversations. I didn't really want to hear any more, but I told her to (e.) **go ahead** anyway. She said that women look for support in conversations. So I asked her what she (f.) **was driving at** when she asked me to go dancing—whether she wanted a little support, or not. In the end, she did say she was looking for support.

Boy, things get very confusing with women. Why don't they just say what they mean? Anyway, it really bothered me that she had already (g.) **talked** it **over** with the other couple and had already decided to go before she asked me. Why didn't she say, "Peter, Kathi, and I have talked about going dancing. We all want to go. We hope you'll come, too." Then things would have been clear, and I still could have said no.

____ 1. continue with something

____ 2. completed, finished

____ 3. Stop behaving that way!

____ 4. was suggesting, was trying to say

____ 5. discussed, considered

____ 6. introduced the topic

____ 7. joking with someone, tricking someone

5. Match It Up Read each line of a telephone conversation between two women. Barbara is telling her friend Sandra about her new boyfriend. Sandra doesn't say much; she mostly paraphrases what Barbara says and gives support. With a partner, write the letter of each of Sandra's responses next to Barbara's lines.

FOR AN EXTRA CHALLENGE: One student reads each of Barbara's lines. The other student finds and reads Sandra's line with the same meaning.

BARBARA:

____ 1. Bill's great. We **get along** so well.

____ 2. He **talks** everything **over** with me before he makes a decision.

____ 3. But last night, he really **threw** me **off** when he told me he owned three homes and he wanted to buy another one.

____ 4. I thought he was **putting** me **on**.

____ 5. Would you **hold on**? I'm getting another call.

____ 6. Sorry that took so long. Where was I? Let me **start over**.

SANDRA:

a. That would have surprised and confused me, too.

b. Sure. I can wait.

c. It's so nice that you have a good relationship.

d. Oh, no, you're not going to begin again, are you?

e. It's great that he discusses everything with you.

f. Well, was he joking or not?

6. Figure It Out Mark the answer that is closest in meaning to each idiom. Compare answers with a partner and try to agree.

SITUATION I: A man and woman at the woman's apartment

1. Elaine: Look Manny, we've discussed this problem many times before. Do I have to **spell** it **out** for you again?

   a. [ ] send it to   b. [ ] make it clear to   c. [ ] avoid talking about it with

2. Manny: OK, Elaine, what **are** you **driving at**? Do you want to end our relationship, or what?

   a. [ ] are you trying to tell me?   b. [ ] are you so happy about?
   c. [ ] are you going to hit me for?

SITUATION II: One friend tells another he's going to be late driving her to the airport.

3. Helen: **Come on**, Matt! If you don't come and get me right away, we'll never get to the airport on time!
   a. [ ] Stop behaving like that   b. [ ] Drive to my house
   c. [ ] You're so slow

4. Matthew: **Take it easy**. We'll get there. All the planes will be late today because of the weather.
   a. [ ] Carry my bags for me.   b. [ ] Have a pill.   c. [ ] Relax.

SITUATION III: Two people in a restaurant

5. David: Rebecca, every time I try to say something, you **cut** me **off**. It's very annoying.
   a. [ ] insult me   b. [ ] stop me   c. [ ] disagree with me

6. Rebecca: Really? It's the first time you've **brought** it **up**. Sorry.
   a. [ ] said something about it   b. [ ] complained about it
   c. [ ] explained how you felt about it

SITUATION IV: A father and daughter in the kitchen

7. Daughter: **Go ahead**, tell me what you think of Jeff. I know he's a little strange.
   a. [ ] Speak, proceed   b. [ ] Leave me alone   c. [ ] Sit, relax

8. Father: Frankly, **I'm at a loss for words**. Ask your mother what she thinks.
   a. [ ] am disappointed   b. [ ] don't know what to say   c. [ ] am pleased

SITUATION V: A woman and her boyfriend

9. Suzanne: If you're trying to **talk** me **into** living with you, you're not doing a very good job.
   a. [ ] ask me about   b. [ ] convince me about   c. [ ] dissuade me from

10. George: Suzanne, **lighten up**. I'm just asking what you think about it.
    a. [ ] lose some weight   b. [ ] be quiet   c. [ ] don't be so serious

7. Choose the Right Card With a partner, choose a greeting card for each situation below.

a. Come on! You're not still angry, are you?

b. We could start over . . .

c. You talked me into it . . .

d. Why don't we talk it over . . .

____ 1. When Joe saw Laurel flirting with another man, he started a fight that ended their relationship. But now, Joe is unhappy about what he did. He wants to begin the relationship again. He sent Laurel this card.

____ 2. Max wants to have a very small wedding, but Vera wants to invite her whole family and all her friends. Vera finally decides that Max is right; there are some good reasons to keep the wedding small. She sent him this card to tell him that he had persuaded her.

____ 3. Stuart said he didn't want Jessica to go to medical school. They didn't talk for a few days. Then she sent him this card.

____ 4. Donna wants her boyfriend to have Thanksgiving dinner with her family, but he doesn't want to. She's upset about it and won't speak to him. He sent her this card.

▶ FOR AN EXTRA CHALLENGE: After the matching activity, on a separate piece of paper write a personal note for the inside of each card. Use idioms from this chapter. Then read your notes to the class.

8. It's News to Me   Read each example of authentic language taken from newspapers and magazines and try to notice the idioms. With a partner, discuss the meaning of each idiom in that particular context. Write the idiom and its meaning below.

1. A headline in *The New York Times*. The article discusses an interview in which Bill Clinton said that Republicans were attacking him personally because they were frustrated that a Democrat had won the presidency and that the American people agreed with his policies.

> *Clinton to Republicans: "Lighten Up"*

_____ = _____

2. An ad for the 1st Nationwide network bank

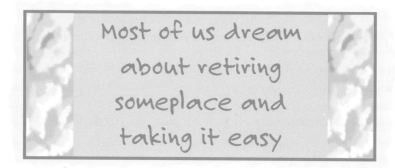

_____ = _____

3. An excerpt from an article in *The New York Times*. The article discusses the reactions of women with breast cancer to various treatments.

> But Ms. Bowers's doctor, Dr. Joyce O'Shaughnessy, a breast cancer specialist at Baylor, did not recommend a bone-marrow transplant. Dr. O'Shaughnessy recommended that Ms. Bowers go ahead with the less extreme chemotherapy program and wait for the results of several major bone-marrow transplant studies before deciding whether to have a transplant.

_____ = _____

4. An excerpt from an article in *The New York Times*. The article discusses former Senator Bill Bradley's decision to run for president.

> Even so, Mr. Bradley, who retired from the Senate in 1996, has resisted requests to put forward many specifics about what he would do as President. He has been reluctant, for example, to spell out how the Administration should be handling the most pressing matter of the day: the crisis in Kosovo.

_____ = _____

▶ GETTING IT RIGHT

9. **Where Do You Put "It"?**   Read each sentence. If the pronoun object is in the right position, mark *OK*. If the pronoun object is in the wrong position, write in the correct phrase. Compare answers with a partner and try to agree.

1. We shouldn't have to spell <u>it</u> out for you at this point.

   OK [ ]   Correction: _____

2. The instructor cut off <u>him</u> because she needed time to discuss the homework.

   OK [ ]   Correction: _____

3. Don't believe anything she says. She's always putting on <u>us</u>.

   OK [ ]   Correction: _____

4. I know it's a big move. Why don't you talk <u>it</u> over with your family?

   OK [ ]   Correction: _____

5. I know it's a little early to bring <u>this</u> up, but when is the final exam?

   OK [ ]   Correction: _____

10. Game: Race to Finish the Idiom Work in groups of four. Student 1 reads each sentence out loud. Students 2, 3, and 4 close their books and listen to each sentence. As quickly as possible, they must say the missing word. (Student 1 keeps score. The answers are on page 184.) The first person to finish the idiom correctly gets one point. The winner is the student with the most points.

SCORING

Student 2 _____ Points _____

Student 3 _____ Points _____

Student 4 _____ Points _____

EXAMPLE: Everybody wants to begin work on the new project, but we still have the old project to wrap ____up____ .

1. I don't know why they got married. They fight all the time. They really don't get _____ .

2. I'm sorry, sir, you'll have to wait a minute. Please hold _____ .

3. You can't possibly cancel the wedding at this late date! Come _____ !

4. Before we actually buy the car, we should talk it _____ .

5. Sherry doesn't believe anything Henry says. She thinks he's putting her _____ .

6. This report is very confusing. Maybe we should start _____ .

7. It's impossible to have a conversation with you! You're always cutting me _____ .

8. Don't be so serious! Lighten _____ .

9. Why did you wait until the end of the meeting to bring this _____ ?

10. What are you trying to tell me? What are you driving _____ ?

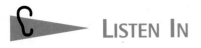

LISTEN IN

11. Listen and Paraphrase Listen to each short conversation between students. Mark the statement that correctly paraphrases what was said.

1. a. [ ] The woman wants the man to say he's sorry for interrupting her.
   b. [ ] The man finishes what he was going to say.
   c. [ ] The woman is sorry she stopped the man while he was speaking.

2. a. [ ] The man wants the woman to change the topic to something more pleasant.
   b. [ ] The man wants to know why the woman is telling him these stories.
   c. [ ] The man wants to hear one horror story after another.

3. a. [ ] After the woman explains why she can't help, the man still wants her to help him.
   b. [ ] The man tells the woman it will be easy to help with the party preparations.
   c. [ ] The man accepts the woman's reason for not helping and tells her to relax.

4. a. [ ] The woman thinks it's necessary to finish the first draft that night to complete the project on time.
   b. [ ] The woman thinks it's necessary to complete the whole project that night.
   c. [ ] The woman thinks it's necessary to continue working on the first draft for another week.

5. a. [ ] The woman doesn't know where the man is driving her.
   b. [ ] The woman doesn't know what the man is trying to tell her.
   c. [ ] The woman has to work like everybody else.

Check your answers in the Answer Key on page 184. For ones you found difficult, read the Tapescript on page 173.

12. Listen and Answer The following conversations take place at a university. Listen to each conversation and the question that follows it. Read the three choices below and mark the one that answers the question correctly.

1. a. [ ] He studied really hard, but was so nervous before the test that he didn't do well.
   b. [ ] It was hard to study for the test.
   c. [ ] He was so shocked by the first question that he couldn't answer any of the questions.

2. a. [ ] He's sorry he hasn't returned the books.
   b. [ ] He's so surprised he thinks she must be joking.
   c. [ ] He wants to discuss his fine with the librarian.

3. a. [ ] They don't know what to do for their American history project.
   b. [ ] They don't really like each other. They have a bad relationship.
   c. [ ] The project is too long. They can't finish it on time.

4. a. [ ] He decided to talk to Professor Greenwood about the psychology course.
   b. [ ] He decided to take the psychology course anyway.
   c. [ ] He decided to take an art course because his friend convinced him to.

5. a. [ ] She wants him to make a few small changes and continue writing the paper.
   b. [ ] She thinks he should begin again, limit the focus, and show her a new outline.
   c. [ ] She thinks he should investigate all the social classes in television sitcoms.

Check your answers in the Answer Key on page 184. For ones you found difficult, read the Tapescript on pages 173-174.

 ## SPEAK UP

13. **Let's Get Personal**   Is this you? For each statement, circle *True* or *False*. Share your answers in a small group. Are the other students in your group just like you?

   1. I'm easy to get along with.   True   False

   2. I get angry when somebody cuts me off in the middle of a story.   True   False

   3. I don't like it when my wife (husband/girlfriend/boyfriend) brings up the topic of money.   True   False

   4. People are always telling me to take it easy.   True   False

   5. I usually like to talk things over before making an important decision.   True   False

   6. I don't like it when I'm on the telephone and the other person asks me to hold on.   True   False

   7. I don't mind starting over—whether it's a new job, new relationship, or new home.   True   False

   8. I'm usually very serious, so my friends are always telling me to lighten up.   True   False

   9. I don't like to have unfinished business, so I'm always glad when I wrap a project up.   True   False

   10. It's not easy to talk me into doing something.   True   False

   FOR AN EXTRA CHALLENGE: After sharing your answers, go back and circle the idiom in each sentence. Check your answers in the Answer Key on page 184.

14. **Act It Out: A Support Group**   In groups of three, act out the conversations. One person presents a problem to the group. The others make suggestions for solving the problem using as many idioms as they can. (Some idioms are given after each situation.) Make any changes you find necessary, for example, change *he* to *she*.

Problem 1: I want to talk about my situation at work. I have a new boss who's a difficult person. He wants everything in a hurry. He gets angry easily. He doesn't explain things clearly. But I really like the work, and I want to stay at that company. I don't know what to do. I don't know whether I should try to discuss it with him or not.

Idioms: bring up, get along with, lighten up, spell out, take it easy, talk over, throw off

Problem 2: My fiancée never says what she wants but then gets angry if I don't do what she wants. Oh, of course, she leaves little hints, but I wish she would be more direct with me.

Idioms: be driving at, bring up, go ahead, spell out, start over, talk over, throw off

Problem 3: I'm dating someone I like, but when we meet friends for dinner, he starts telling these stories about work and he won't stop. It can be very boring.

Idioms: bring up, cut off, go ahead, hold on, lighten up, spell out, start over, take it easy, talk over

WRITE IT OUT

15. **Create a Conversation**   Look at the two cartoons. Choose the one that interests you. Find a partner who chose the same cartoon. Together, write a conversation for your cartoon, using as many idioms as you can from the list on pages 15–16. You can also use the captions (the words below the drawings) in your conversation. Then read your conversation to the class.

"Your allowance[2] is in the mail."

"I can highly recommend the peanut-butter-and-jelly sandwich, served with a chilled glass of milk."

[2] *allowance:* spending money parents give their children once a week or once a month

LOOK IT OVER

16. Review the Idioms   With a partner, decide which of the activities below will help you learn the most.

- Write the meaning of each idiom.

- Write a sample sentence for each idiom.

- Give examples of subjects and/or objects that go with each idiom.
  (Note: Not all idioms require objects.)

    EXAMPLE: <u>This class</u> has almost wrapped up <u>this chapter</u>.
    s o

- Practice saying the idioms with correct stress. (Verbs and adverbs/particles are stressed, but the verbs *to be* and *to have* and one-syllable prepositions are not stressed.) If possible, practice saying the idioms in sentences.

Then use the list that follows to help you complete the activities together. Note the two symbols for objects.

( ) = The object of the preposition. It goes after the preposition.

[ ] = The object of the phrasal verb. If it is a pronoun, it goes between the verb and adverb/particle. If it is a noun, it can go between the verb and the adverb/particle *or* after the adverb/particle.

---

1. be at a loss for words _____

   _____

2. be driving at _____

   _____

   Usage: Informal; usually with what: What are you driving at?

3. bring [ ] up; bring [ ] up with ( ) _____

   _____

4. come on _____

   _____

   Usage: Informal; imperative only: Come on!

5. cut [ ] off _____

   _____

6. get along; get along with ( ) _____

   _____

7. go ahead; go ahead with ( ) _____

_____

8. hold on _____

_____

9. lighten up _____

_____

10. put [ ] on _____

_____
Usage: Informal

11. spell [ ] out; spell [ ] out for ( ) _____

_____

12. start over _____

_____

13. take it easy _____

_____
Usage: Informal

14. talk [ ] into ( ) _____

_____
Usage: The object of *into* can be a gerund: *They talked us into going to Oregon.*

15. talk [ ] over; talk [ ] over with ( ) _____

_____

16. throw [ ] off _____

_____
Usage: Informal

17. wrap up; wrap [ ] up _____

_____
Usage: Informal

Chapter 2 BUSINESS

GETTING STARTED

1. **Answer the Survey** Write your answers to the following survey questions. Then interview a partner and write his or her answers. Discuss your answers.

My answers	My partner's answers
1. Do you know anything about the company called Microsoft? [ ] Yes. What do you know? _____ _____ [ ] No.	1. Do you know anything about the company called Microsoft? [ ] Yes. What do you know? _____ _____ [ ] No.
2. Do you know about any other successful companies? [ ] Yes. Which ones? _____ _____ [ ] No.	2. Do you know about any other successful companies? [ ] Yes. Which ones? _____ _____ [ ] No.
3. Check the three things you think are necessary for starting a company: [ ] money [ ] good ideas [ ] a partner you trust [ ] computers and other equipment [ ] business experience [ ] training in economics [ ] a marketing plan [ ] courage [ ] willingness to work hard	3. Check the three things you think are necessary for starting a company: [ ] money [ ] good ideas [ ] a partner you trust [ ] computers and other equipment [ ] business experience [ ] training in economics [ ] a marketing plan [ ] courage [ ] willingness to work hard

INTRODUCTION OF IDIOMS

2. **Read Between the Lines**   Read the corporate profile. With a partner, try to understand what it says. Then do Exercise 3.

MICROSOFT: CASHING IN ON SOFTWARE AND THE INTERNET

MICROSOFT AT A GLANCE[1]

- Microsoft is the first personal computer software company to have over a billion dollars in sales in one year.
- One hundred million copies of Windows[2] have already been **shipped out**.
- Products are available in over thirty languages, and international sales **make up** more than half the revenues.

CHAIRMAN AND CHIEF EXECUTIVE OFFICER: WILLIAM H. GATES III

Bill Gates was born in 1955 in Seattle, Washington. His father was an attorney, his mother a school teacher. Gates attended a public elementary school and a private high school. In 1973, he entered Harvard University as a freshman. At the time, computers were enormous machines called mainframes and were used mostly by government and business. Personal computers (PCs) **were** not **on the market** yet.

In 1975, Bill Gates and his friend Paul Allen saw an article in a magazine about a PC called the Altair. Sensing the potential of PCs, they **worked out** the first computer language program for a PC. They called it BASIC and sold it to the company that made the Altair. Later that year, Bill Gates left school to develop software full-time.

THE COMPANY'S HISTORY

In 1975, Bill Gates and Paul Allen **set up** Microsoft, a computer software company, in New Mexico. Gates improved BASIC, then **did business with** new clients, such as Citibank and General Electric. By 1977, Gates and Allen officially formed a partnership and began to **build up** their software business.

By 1978, Gates and Allen had adapted two computer languages for the PC, FORTRAN and COBOL. By year's end, their belief in the PC had **paid off**: The company had sold over a million dollars' worth of software products.

Microsoft moved to the state of Washington and in 1981 was reorganized into a privately held corporation. Bill Gates became president and chairman of the board; Paul Allen was named executive vice president. Two years later, Allen **bowed out of** Microsoft but remains on its Board of Directors.

After introducing Microsoft Word[3] and Microsoft Windows, the company **took off**. By its tenth anniversary (in 1985), Microsoft was really **cashing in on** its software. The company was **making money**, big money. Sales were $140 million.

The company went public in 1986, with stock selling at $21.00 a share. This raised $61 million in cash. Soon, Microsoft was **branching out** into publishing, consulting, multimedia, on-line encyclopedias, and even language instruction. As part of this expansion, it **bought out** other companies with innovative ideas.

THE VISION FOR THE FUTURE

While Microsoft will continue to **put out** software for the PC, the company **changed course** near the end of the twentieth century. It's now **betting on** Internet-related technologies that offer more knowledge and power to those who **surf the Net**.

---

[1] As of 1996

[2] *Windows*: software that lets a user view different application programs at the same time; Windows® is a registered trademark of Microsoft Inc.

[3] *Microsoft Word*®: a word-processing program; Word® is a registered trademark of Microsoft Inc.

3. Line by Line With a partner, mark the answer that explains the corporate profile on page 18. Then look at the corporate profile and find the sentence with the same meaning. Write that sentence below.

1. How do we know that the Microsoft product Windows has been successful?

   a. [ ] Millions of copies have been made.

   b. [ ] It was made for the first PC called the Altair.

   c. [ ] Millions of them have been sent to customers.

   Sentence: _____

2. In 1973, when Gates was a freshman at Harvard, were personal computers (PCs) being sold?

   a. [ ] Yes, they were available to everybody.

   b. [ ] No, they were not being sold at that time.

   c. [ ] Yes, but they were used mostly by companies and government offices.

   Sentence: _____

3. Did Paul Allen keep his job as executive vice president at Microsoft?

   a. [ ] Yes, he continued as executive vice president for many years.

   b. [ ] No, he became president after two years at Microsoft.

   c. [ ] No, he left his job but is still a member of the Board of Directors.

   Sentence: _____

4. What happened to Microsoft after it began to sell Microsoft Word and Microsoft Windows?

   a. [ ] Business got much better.

   b. [ ] Business got much worse.

   c. [ ] Business stayed the same.

   Sentence: _____

5. By 1985, what was happening at Microsoft?

   a. [ ] The company was benefiting from its software products.

   b. [ ] The company needed cash to survive.

   c. [ ] The company was sold for 140 million dollars.

   Sentence: _____

6. What was the financial situation at Microsoft by its tenth anniversary?

   a. [ ] The company was selling a lot of products but didn't have a lot of cash.

   b. [ ] The products were bringing a lot of money to the company.

   c. [ ] The products were selling at low prices.

   Sentence: _____

7. Did Microsoft continue to make software for the PC, move into new areas, or both?

    a. [ ] The company continued to make software for the PC. That's all.

    b. [ ] The company moved into new areas such as publishing. That's all.

    c. [ ] The company continued to make software and also moved into new areas.

    Sentence: _____

8. Which statement is true of Microsoft at the end of the twentieth century?

    a. [ ] The company will stop producing software for the PC.

    b. [ ] The company will continue to produce software for the PC.

    c. [ ] The company expects to make money from surfing and gambling.

    Sentence: _____

4. Paraphrase the E-mail Message   Read the e-mail message below. Work with a partner. For each idiom in bold, find the meaning in the box. Write the letter of the idiom next to its meaning.

> Lexie,
>
> I got your message about investing in Netsurf. This is the first chance I've had to e-mail my reply. No, I don't think it's too late to buy Netsurf stock. I think it'll really (a.) **pay off** in the next few years. The company has (b.) **bought out** a bunch of innovative businesses. It's (c.) **branching out** in exciting directions. Because you like to (d.) **surf the Net,** Netsurf's new products for the Internet will probably interest you. (I'll try to send you some literature on these.) Also, overseas sales (e.) **make up** more than 50 percent of Netsurf's income. This shows that the company's products are doing well all over the world. I know you've been avoiding computer stocks because you think they're risky. Frankly, I think it's time for you to (f.) **change course**. I'm (g.) **betting on** Netsurf. Maybe you should, too.
>
> Chris

____ 1. go in a different direction

____ 2. purchased 100 percent of

____ 3. expanding in

____ 4. be profitable, be worthwhile

____ 5. represent, compose

____ 6. taking a chance on and expecting
       to be successful with

____ 7. look for information on the Internet

5. Understanding a Biographical Statement   Read the biographical statement. Work with a partner. For each idiom in bold, find the meaning in the box at the right. Write the letter of the idiom next to its meaning.

BIOGRAPHICAL STATEMENT
FOR WILLIAM H. GATES III

In 1975, William H. Gates (a.) **set up** Microsoft with Paul Allen in New Mexico. Their first customer was the company that made the PC called the Altair, but they also (b.) **did business with** Citibank and General Electric.

They (c.) **worked out** computer languages for the early PCs. This is how they (d.) **built up** their software business.

In 1983, Paul Allen (e.) **bowed out of** the company, but Gates continued as president and chairman of the board. Because of Microsoft, Gates became the richest man in the world.

____ 1. sold products to, worked for or with

____ 2. left quietly, quit

____ 3. developed and solved the problems of

____ 4. established, organized

____ 5. expanded, made grow

NEW CONTEXTS

6. Figure It Out   Mark the answer that is closest in meaning to each idiom. Compare answers with a partner and try to agree.

SITUATION I: Husband and wife at the breakfast table

1. Wife: I don't like my job anymore. I think the best thing to do is **bow out** in the next month or two.

   a. [ ] stay and be quiet   b. [ ] wait to be fired   c. [ ] leave the job quietly

2. Husband: With your experience, all you need to do is **surf the Net** and you'll find plenty of jobs.

   a. [ ] spend time at the beach   b. [ ] search on the Internet
   c. [ ] send out your resume

3. Interviewer: So, is it true that you're going to **change course** and develop electric cars?

    a. [ ] continue in the same direction　　b. [ ] go in a new direction
    c. [ ] close the factories

4. Executive: Yes, we hope our first electric car will **be on the market** in two years.

    a. [ ] be in the design phase　　b. [ ] be ready to be sold
    c. [ ] be very successful

SITUATION III: Two television executives discussing the company's future

5. Wendy: Frankly, I think we should **buy out** some small television stations now.

    a. [ ] invest some money in　　b. [ ] purchase 100 percent of　　c. [ ] close

6. Craig: I disagree. I think we should **cash in on** our success and put the money in the bank.

    a. [ ] advertise　　b. [ ] be quiet about　　c. [ ] get the money from

SITUATION IV: At the end of a business meeting

7. Kelly: Well, it's been a pleasure **doing business with** you.

    a. [ ] working with　　b. [ ] meeting　　c. [ ] introducing the company to

8. Arnold: I'm sure we will both **make money** in the very near future.

    a. [ ] pay the bills　　b. [ ] work hard　　c. [ ] earn a profit

SITUATION V: Two editors at a publishing company

9. Victoria: It looks as if everybody is **betting on** our new writer.

    a. [ ] enjoying reading　　b. [ ] expecting success from　　c. [ ] talking to

10. Laurence: Well, we'll soon see. We just **shipped out** sixty thousand copies of his novel.

    a. [ ] printed　　b. [ ] bought　　c. [ ] sent

SITUATION VI: Two teachers at an English-language institute

11. Craig: We may lose students because of the economic crisis in Asia. You know, students from that part of the world normally **make up** 40 percent of our enrollment.

    a. [ ] need to be　　b. [ ] represent, compose　　c. [ ] help us reach

12. Elizabeth: If that happens, we'll have to do a lot of advertising to **build up** the program again.

    a. [ ] construct a new home for　　b. [ ] tell people about
    c. [ ] steadily make larger

7. Who's Who? With a partner, match the names of famous people with the descriptions. When you are finished, share your answers with the class.

___ 1. This woman attracted a television audience of 33 million and **cashed in on** the obsession with self-help in the United States.

___ 2. This internationally known cellist has **put out** several classical albums.

___ 3. This woman established a women's fashion company that **branched out** and now makes clothes for men and children as well as women.

___ 4. This man **bet on** television news. In 1980, he created CNN, a television station that offers news programs twenty-four hours a day. In 1997, he donated $1 billion to the United Nations.

___ 5. In 1997, this golfer's training and practice really **paid off**. He became the youngest golfer to win the Masters Tournament.

___ 6. This woman **set up** a company called The Body Shop, which sells shampoos, lotions, and creams with natural ingredients from isolated parts of South America. The company also sends some of its profits back to those countries.

___ 7. This female singer **built up** a following and sold more than 100 million albums worldwide, including *Material Girl*. She is head of her own record company and has an estimated fortune of $200 million.

___ 8. This man created *Star Wars*, a series of science-fiction films that really **took off**. They rank among the most financially successful movies of all time.

a. Ted Turner

b. Madonna

c. Yo Yo Ma

d. Oprah Winfrey

e. George Lucas

f. Tiger Woods

g. Anita Roddick

h. Donna Karan

8. What Would *You* Do?   Read each situation and mark your answer. Share your answers in a small group. One student in each group reports the results to the class.

1. You are a manager in a clothing store. You hired six new salespeople because you expected business to **take off** before the holidays, but it didn't. What will you do?

   a. [ ] Fire the employees right away.
   b. [ ] Wait for the new employees to quit, but fire them if they don't.
   c. [ ] Tell the employees they must quit but help them get jobs at other companies.
   d. [ ] Other: _____

2. You were hired by a software company to **work out** the problems in its new product. The product must **be on the market** by September before the competitors begin to sell their products. You now realize you can't finish by the deadline and the product will be late. What will you do?

   a. [ ] Don't say anything. Continue working.
   b. [ ] Tell your boss the product will not be ready by September.
   c. [ ] Ask to hire an assistant and try to finish on time.
   d. [ ] Other: _____

3. A client you **do business with** is still trying to date you after you've said no many times. You know the client is very important to your company, but you don't want to get romantically involved with this person. What will you do?

   a. [ ] Don't say anything to your boss. Continue to say no to the client.
   b. [ ] Tell your boss you can't work with this client anymore. Explain why.
   c. [ ] Tell your boss you can't work with this client anymore. Don't explain why.
   d. [ ] Other: _____

4. You're thinking about leaving your job, and you're looking for a new job. Yesterday, your boss found you **surfing the Net** for other jobs. What will you do?

   a. [ ] Pretend that you were trying to help a friend find a job. Don't admit that the job was for you.
   b. [ ] Say you just wanted to see what the salaries were at other companies.
   c. [ ] Tell the truth even if it means getting fired.
   d. [ ] Other: _____

5. You've been working for a toy company for two years, and you like your job. You also need the job to support your family. Recently, however, you've discovered that one of the toys the company **puts out** isn't safe for children. What will you do?

   a. [ ] Don't say anything.
   b. [ ] Tell your boss and do whatever he or she wants to do.
   c. [ ] Tell your boss and say you can't work there if the company doesn't correct the problem.
   d. [ ] Other: _____

9. Where Do You Put "It"?   Read each sentence. If the pronoun object is in the right position, mark *OK*. If the pronoun object is in the wrong position, write in the correct phrase. Compare answers with a partner and try to agree.

1. The company is doing poorly. They have to build up <u>it</u> right away, or it will fail.

   OK [ ]   Correction: _____

2. If I were you, I wouldn't bet on <u>it</u>.

   OK [ ]   Correction: _____

3. She doesn't want to run the restaurant anymore. She's hoping someone will buy <u>her</u> out this year.

   OK [ ]   Correction: _____

4. Have you seen Sony's latest televisions? They're shipping out <u>them</u> this month.

   OK [ ]   Correction: _____

5. Carlos was the only one who could solve the engineering problem. He worked out <u>it</u> in two days.

   OK [ ]   Correction: _____

LISTEN IN

10. Listen and Answer   The following is an interview with the CEO (chief executive officer) of Super Sunglasses. Listen to each part of the interview and the question that follows it. Read the three choices below and mark the one that answers the question correctly.

1. a. [ ] People paid cash for sunglasses, especially good sunglasses.
   b. [ ] The woman couldn't find any good sunglasses for her lens shop.
   c. [ ] The woman wanted to profit from the interest in sunglasses.

2. a. [ ] The company was successful from the beginning. It was a good investment.
   b. [ ] The company has not been financially successful so far. The CEO is still repaying the money she borrowed to start the business, but she hopes to do well.
   c. [ ] The company is in danger of closing. The CEO's investment was a big mistake.

3. a. [ ] If the company will open new stores to sell its sunglasses
   b. [ ] If the company will sell other products besides sunglasses
   c. [ ] What the woman was thinking about during the interview

4. a. [ ] The plan is to make stronger sunglasses so they don't break easily.
   b. [ ] The plan is to move the company to a new building.
   c. [ ] The plan is to increase the number and type of sunglasses offered.

5. a. [ ] The companies are in the United States, Latin America, and Japan.
   b. [ ] Only companies outside the United States buy her sunglasses.
   c. [ ] Only companies in the United States buy her sunglasses.

Check your answers in the Answer Key on page 185. For ones you found difficult, read the Tapescript on page 174.

11. Listen, Take Notes, and Answer   Listen to the lecture in a college course in business. The professor is presenting a true case of a self-made man. Take notes while you listen. Then answer the questions.

1. What does the professor discuss?
   a. [ ] How a teenager from New York **bet on** the lawn-care business and became a multimillionaire.
   b. [ ] How a boy who cut grass started cleaning offices and **built up** a multimillion-dollar cleaning business.
   c. [ ] How another company **bought out** Laro Service Systems and made Robert Bertuglia a multimillionaire in the 1980s.

2. According to the professor, what helped Bertuglia's business grow? (*Mark two answers.*)
   a. [ ] He **changed course** from lawn care to cleaning services when the opportunity presented itself.
   b. [ ] He **bought out** other companies that cleaned commercial buildings and hired their employees.
   c. [ ] He **cashed in on** the national trend away from higher-paid union workers to lower-paid non-union workers.

3. What was the status of Laro Service Systems by the end of the 1990s?
   a. [ ] It was just being **set up** at that point by Robert Bertuglia.
   b. [ ] It was **branching out** into cleaning homes in addition to offices.
   c. [ ] It was **doing business with** so many companies that it had become one of the largest, private building-service companies in New York.

4. What happened to Bertuglia as his company grew?
   a. [ ] He **bowed out** of the company after working seven days a week, fifty-two weeks a year for over twenty years.
   b. [ ] He spent so much time at work as his business **took off** that he lost his marriage and his dream house.
   c. [ ] His hard work **paid off** at work and at home.

Compare answers with a partner and try to agree. If you need to, look at the Tapescript on page 175.

SPEAK UP

12. Let's Get Personal   Is this you? For each statement, circle *True* or *False*. Share your answers in a small group. Are the other students in your group just like you?

1. I'm practical. I think it's important to study a subject that will pay off when I finish school.   True   False

2. I really want to make a lot of money.   True   False

3. I'm the type of person who likes to change course every few years—for example, find a new job, live in a different place, attend a new school.   True   False

4. I don't like to spend time working out the solutions to difficult problems. I get frustrated if I can't solve a problem quickly.   True   False

5. I wouldn't like to start a business. I'm happy to take a job after everything has already been set up.   True   False

6. I never surf the Net.   True   False

7. I have some good ideas for a new business. Some day I hope to cash in on my ideas.   True   False

8. I'd like to work for a company that puts out a high-quality product.   True   False

9. If I had problems with my partner in a business, I would probably bow out and let him or her run the company alone.   True   False

10. I usually buy new products as soon as they are on the market.   True   False

FOR AN EXTRA CHALLENGE: After sharing your answers, go back and circle the idiom in each sentence. Check your answers in the Answer Key on page 185.

13. Act It Out: Job Interviews   Read the ads below. Find at least three jobs or business opportunities that interest you. Then prepare questions about the company, using as many idioms as you can from the list on pages 30–31. Then, with your partner playing a company representative, role-play a phone conversation in which you respond to the ad.

HELP WANTED

1.

SALESPEOPLE NEEDED
for a furniture company that's starting to take off.
Call Marie: 555-3222

2.

Latin American countries make up 40% of our business. Spanish-speaking managers needed. 555-5432

3. Make money through your hobby. If you surf the Net for fun, join our medical research firm and surf the Net for big bucks.
Call today: 555-7688

4. **CASH IN ON YOUR LOVE OF BOOKS.**
Readers needed at major publisher.
Phone: 555-8999

5. **SUMMER WORK**
for college students. We put out high-quality software for computer graphics.
KVTV: 555-9000

6. School bus company currently building up its West Coast division. Account executives needed. Must be willing to relocate.
Day Buses: 555-5111

BUSINESS OPPORTUNITIES

7. Investors needed for entertainment co. that's branching out. Call: Marcia Miller, Director, CIN, 555–1000, ext. 85

8. Investors needed for a sporting shoe manufacturer which is about to change course.
Contact: Manuel Lopez, 555–3000

WRITE IT OUT

14. Create a Corporate Profile   Read the details below on Ethan Allen Interiors Inc. Then, with a partner, use the details to write a profile of the company. Use as many idioms as you can from the list on pages 30–31.

- Ethan Allen manufactures and sells quality home furnishings through a network of over 300 retail stores.
- The company's products include furniture, upholstery, and accessories that are available in classic and casual collections.
- Sales, evenly divided between the classic and casual styles, increased 12.2 percent in the last year. The company spent over 68 million dollars on advertising, established new stores, and moved some stores to different locations. It also invested in new machinery that has increased production and sped the delivery of products.
- Recent innovations include:
  - offering new products such as E.A. Kids™, a collection for the children's market;
  - using new technologies to design products and process orders;
  - creating a website so consumers can shop for home furnishings on the Internet.
- The Ethan Allen network includes 288 stores located across the United States, 21 stores overseas, and "12,000 professionals dedicated to providing consumers with an exceptional shopping experience."

Source: The 1998 Annual Report by M. Farooq Kathwari, Chairman, President and Chief Executive Officer, Ethan Allen Interiors Inc.

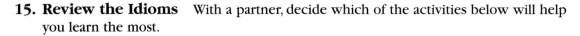

15. Review the Idioms   With a partner, decide which of the activities below will help you learn the most.

- Write the meaning of each idiom.

- Write a sample sentence for each idiom.

- Give examples of subjects and/or objects that go with each idiom.
  (Note: Not all idioms require objects.)

  EXAMPLE: <u>This class</u> has almost wrapped up <u>this chapter</u>.
                S   O

- Practice saying the idioms with correct stress. (Verbs and adverbs/particles are stressed, but the verbs *to be* and *to have* and one-syllable prepositions are not stressed.) If possible, practice saying the idioms in sentences.

Then use the list that follows to help you complete the activities together. Note the two symbols for objects.

( ) = The object of the preposition. It goes after the preposition.
[ ] = The object of the phrasal verb. If it is a pronoun, it goes between the verb and adverb/particle. If it is a noun, it can go between the verb and the adverb/particle *or* after the adverb/particle.

1. be on the market; go on the market _____

_____

2. bet on ( ) _____

_____

3. bow out; bow out of ( ) _____

_____

4. branch out _____

_____

5. build [ ] up; build [ ] up into ( ) _____

_____

6. buy [ ] out _____

_____

7. cash in on ( ) _____

_____
Usage: Informal

8. change course _____

_____
Usage: Informal

9. do business with ( ) _____

_____

10. make money _____

_____

11. make up ( ) _____

_____

12. pay off _____

_____

13. put [ ] out _____

_____

14. set [ ] up _____

_____

15. ship [ ] out _____

_____

16. surf the Net[4] _____

_____

17. take off _____

_____

18. work [ ] out _____

_____

---

[4] *Net*: an informal, short form for Internet

3 RESIDENCE

GETTING STARTED

1. **Share Your Reactions**   In a small group, discuss the following statistics about the United States. Compare these facts with the situation in your country. Share your reactions with the class.

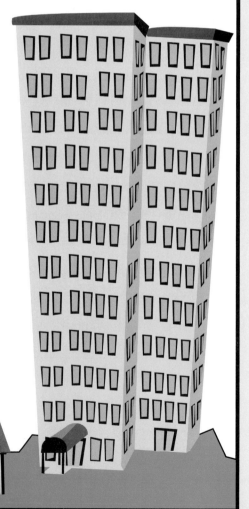

Homes in the United States

- People in the United States live in an average of 30 different homes in their lifetime.
- Of the 98 million households in the United States, 65 percent own their home or apartment.
- People who live alone represent 25 percent of all households in the United States today. In 1970, this group was 12 percent.
- At the end of the 20th century, about 78 percent of the U.S. population lived in metropolitan areas (31% in central cities; 47% in suburbs). About 22 percent lived in rural areas.
- In the United States, lawns occupy more land than wheat, corn, tobacco, or any other single crop.

INTRODUCTION OF IDIOMS

2. Read Between the Lines Read the newspaper article. With a partner, try to understand what it means. Then do Exercise 3.

Moving In and Moving Out: The Housing Boom

Recently, a housing boom has spread across the country. New homes and residential communities are appearing almost overnight. The healthy economy is the main reason for this boom. Consumers not only have confidence in the country's economy, they also have confidence in their own earning power. They have money to spend and are willing to spend it on a house. Instead of **holding onto** what they have and **fixing** it **up**, many want to buy a bigger home. In fact, for the last few years, Americans have been **moving into** a million new homes a year, an all-time high.

Typical of this trend is the Chicago couple, Dawn and David Smith, and their son, Robbie. With both adults working full-time, they're now ready to buy a home in the suburbs. "We've been **cooped up in** a small apartment long enough," explains Dawn. David says proudly, "With the economy doing well and our personal income up, we feel we can really **take our pick** of available houses." And young Robbie adds, "I'm going to have a finished basement where I can **have** friends **over** and **stay up** late."

This housing boom, however, is not without its problems. In a number of suburbs on the West Coast as well as the East Coast, the demand for housing has pushed prices ridiculously high. In some of these communities, simple two-bedroom houses can cost over half a million dollars. And buyers, hoping to live close to work and concerned that prices might go higher, are afraid to **pass** them **up**.

So while the Smiths feel they have plenty of choices, other families find they must take what they can afford. Nancy Dworkin of Palo Alto, California, tells us, "We had always dreamed of a house **looking out on** the bay, but we just can't afford it." Her husband Steve Dworkin says, "We very much wanted a big kitchen so we could cook together and **eat in** a few nights a week, but a house like that is out of our price range."

To pay for their new house with the three-car garage in Pacific Palisades, California, Keiko and Lance Johnson say they are working longer days, which leaves little time for their two young children. In their "free time," this couple finds they're busy doing chores such as **cleaning out** the garage or **keeping up** the grounds. The time that used to be reserved for family, friends, and neighbors is dwindling.

As new homes bring more people to a community, shopping centers and malls follow. Additional people bring traffic, congestion, and parking lots. Farmland and open spaces are sacrificed to **make room for** all the new developments. In many suburbs, this growth is unplanned and results in what's now called *suburban sprawl*. The quality of life that drew people to these communities in the first place is being lost.

Here and there, people are rejecting the suburban lifestyle. Some are moving to more rural areas where houses are cheaper and they can be closer to nature. Others are actually **moving out of** the suburbs and returning to the cities where they can live in a tiny apartment, **eat out** a lot, and **get around** on foot. They're leaving so that the big house and the busy schedule will no longer dominate their lives.

3. **Line by Line**   With a partner, mark the answer that explains the newspaper article on page 33. Then look at the newspaper article and find the sentence with the same meaning. Write that sentence below.

1. During this good economic time, are Americans keeping their existing homes and making improvements to them?

   a. [ ] Yes, a million people are renovating their homes each year.
   b. [ ] No, they're keeping their homes but not improving them.
   c. [ ] No, they're not improving their existing homes; they're buying new homes.

   Sentence: _____

2. How big is the Smiths' apartment?

   a. [ ] It's too big for their family.
   b. [ ] It's too small for their family.
   c. [ ] It's just right for their family.

   Sentence: _____

3. How does David Smith feel about the housing market in this economy?

   a. [ ] He feels they can choose any house they want.
   b. [ ] He feels there aren't a lot of choices.
   c. [ ] He feels they can't afford a lot of houses.

   Sentence: _____

4. What do buyers do when two-bedroom houses cost more than half a million dollars?

   a. [ ] They walk by and don't look back.
   b. [ ] They're nervous about rejecting them because they fear prices will go even higher.
   c. [ ] They bargain until the price of the house is lowered because they want to live near their job.

   Sentence: _____

5. What does Nancy Dworkin want in her dream house?

   a. [ ] A view of the bay
   b. [ ] Big bedrooms
   c. [ ] A swimming pool

   Sentence: _____

6. What does Nancy's husband, Steve, say they want?

   a. [ ] A house near a lot of restaurants that are within their price range
   b. [ ] A kitchen where they could cook and have their meals
   c. [ ] A cook to prepare meals for them

   Sentence: _____

7. Some people don't want the suburban lifestyle anymore. What are they doing?

a. [ ] Leaving the suburbs for small apartments in the city, and eating in restaurants instead of cooking

b. [ ] Changing their furniture and reorganizing their lives so they can eat at home more with their families

c. [ ] Buying even bigger houses

Sentence: _____

4. **Paraphrase the Arguments**   List A and List B both present arguments against moving to the suburbs. List A contains idioms from this chapter, and List B paraphrases them. Read both lists. With a partner, match each argument in List A with a sentence with a similar meaning from List B. Write the letter of the paraphrase next to each argument in List A.

REASONS NOT TO MOVE TO THE SUBURBS

LIST A. IDIOMS

____ 1. You already have a house you can **fix up**.

____ 2. You'll spend your free time **cleaning out** the garage.

____ 3. You'll also have to spend time **keeping up** the garden.

____ 4. In the suburbs, farmland and open spaces are being sold to **make room for** new houses.

____ 5. In the suburbs, you can't **get around** on foot; you have to have a car.

LIST B. PARAPHRASES

a. To create space for housing developments, open spaces are being sold.

b. You cannot reach different places by walking in the suburbs.

c. It will be necessary to maintain the garden.

d. You can make improvements and repairs to your current house.

e. When you're not working, you'll be emptying the garage, sweeping it, and organizing it.

5. Paraphrase the E-mail Message   After being interviewed about moving to a house, Robbie sends an e-mail message to one of his friends. Read his message. Work with a partner. For each idiom in bold, find the meaning in the box. Write the letter of the idiom next to its meaning.

Subj: shocking news

Date: 00-12-07 17:01:27 EST

From: robdiv@win.com

To: jj@win.com

Hey JoJo,

You won't believe this. My parents are actually discussing (a.) **moving out of** the city and (b.) **moving into** a house in the suburbs. At first, I didn't want to move, but then I started thinking about (c.) **having** a bunch of friends **over** and (d.) **staying up** all night. You can't do that in a tiny apartment in the city. I also have lots of plans for the garage (my own car, jet ski, snowboard, etc.). I never thought I'd say this, but I'm ready for the 'burbs.[1]

Rob

_____ 1. not going to sleep

_____ 2. leaving one's residence permanently

_____ 3. inviting people to visit one's home

_____ 4. starting to live in a new residence

_____

[1] *'burbs*: an informal, short form for *suburbs*

6. Figure It Out   Mark the answer that is closest in meaning to each idiom. Compare answers with a partner and try to agree.

SITUATION I: Two co-workers discussing one's apartment

1. Wanda: When you **move into** that one-bedroom, you'll have a lot more room for your photography and all your other interests.

    a. [ ] begin to look for   b. [ ] begin to live in   c. [ ] begin to build

2. Charles: Yes, but first I have to put everything in boxes and **move out of** this place.

    a. [ ] continue to live in   b. [ ] stop living in   c. [ ] act quickly

SITUATION II: Two friends discussing buying a cooperative apartment

3. Sue: The price is right and the location is great. It would be crazy to **pass** this apartment **up**.

    a. [ ] not take   b. [ ] criticize   c. [ ] walk past

4. Doris: Yes, but it **looks out on** a brick wall. Who wants that?

    a. [ ] resembles   b. [ ] has a view of   c. [ ] needs work on

SITUATION III: Two roommates discussing their ideas for dinner

5. Debbie: We've been spending a lot of money on restaurants lately. Let's **eat in** tonight.

    a. [ ] have dinner at a friend's house   b. [ ] have dinner at home
    c. [ ] find a cheaper place

6. Carol: I don't want to do a lot of cooking and cleaning tonight. I'd prefer to **eat out**.

    a. [ ] have dinner in a restaurant   b. [ ] cook dinner at home
    c. [ ] get a delivery

SITUATION IV: A mother and daughter discussing the arrival of a new baby

7. Mother: This apartment is so small. How will you **make room for** your new baby?

    a. [ ] work at home with   b. [ ] decorate the nursery for   c. [ ] create space for

8. Daughter: We're going to put a window in the walk-in closet and **fix** it **up** as a nursery.

    a. [ ] decorate   b. [ ] build   c. [ ] call

SITUATION V: Friends discussing a house one of them has inherited from his parents

9. George: I don't understand why you're **holding onto** your parents' house. You don't want to live there.

    a. [ ] keeping   b. [ ] renting   c. [ ] renovating

10. Ryan: I'm trying to **keep** it **up** for now and sell it later for a higher price.

    a. [ ] talk to a real estate agent about   b. [ ] plant trees around
    c. [ ] maintain in good condition

7. **Fill in the Missing Words**   Choose either His Point of View (below) or Her Point of View (on pages 39-40).

His Point of View

Two men are relaxing in an office at the end of the workday. One is doing most of the talking. Read what they say. With a partner, write in the word missing in each idiom.

NICK: You know we've been living in the city, but now we have this little country house—her idea. It used to be a church. Can you believe that? I thought we'd stay there once in a while, but no. Every weekend she has to go to the country. Says she feels (1.) cooped_____ in our little apartment, *my* little apartment, from my single days. So now, every Friday, we drive 50 miles, along with all the other commuters, to spend the weekend at the malls or the antique shops. And then it's cleaning, yes, (2.) cleaning_____ the garage, the attic, the basement. I mean, can you imagine? Just what I want to do: spend my weekend driving, shopping, and cleaning. I tried to explain that if we sold the country house, we could travel, (3.) get_____ and see the world: California, Mexico, Bali, Spain, Egypt. . . . But no, she wants to (4.) hold_____ it, (5.) fix it _____, clean its little picture window which (6.) looks_____ on all the neighbors—people, by the way, whose only conversation is about their lawns, their children, and their pets. We (7.) _____ each other over for barbecues. My wife can't (8.) pass_____ an invitation—not one, not a single one—and we (9.) _____up into the night talking about nothing, just trivia.

ROBERTO: I thought that was everything you wanted.

NICK: Not exactly.

Her Point of View

Two women are having lunch at a restaurant. They are friends, but their busy careers and personal lives have prevented them from meeting frequently. Read their conversation. With a partner, write the word missing in each idiom.

ALYSSA: Oh, Nick's fine. He's doing really well, but he's working very hard. He needs more time to relax, so we recently bought a country house.

LAURA: Oh, how wonderful. We're hoping to do the same some day.

ALYSSA: Actually, it was an old church. We just love it. Of course we had to (1.) <u>clean</u>_____ all the pews and whatnot, and it still needs (2.) _____ up, but now we have an eat-in kitchen—something we don't have here in the city.

LAURA: Oh really? Poor you. That was the one thing I insisted on when Roberto and I got married: that we (3.) <u>move</u>_____ a decent apartment. I refused to be (4.) _____ <u>up in</u> a tiny one-bedroom with a kitchen the size of a locker.

ALYSSA: Well, Nick won't (5.) <u>move</u>_____ of his old village apartment. He says he loves the neighborhood . . . and because the place is so cheap, we'll (6.) _____ onto it and save money for other things. OK, I said, then we can use the money for a country retreat.

LAURA: Good for you! You have to say what you want.

ALYSSA: Oh, absolutely. I agree. You know, in our city apartment, there's no room to entertain. In the country, we've been having barbecues, but we're enlarging our kitchen and (7.) _____ <u>room for</u> a big table. That way, we'll be able to (8.) <u>have</u> friends _____ for more formal dinners.

LAURA: Well, we've been (9.) <u>fixing</u>_____ our place, too. We have a new picture window on the west side of the building, so the dining room (10.) _____ <u>out on</u> the park now.

ALYSSA: Divine! I'd love to see it.

LAURA: Well, I'd love to (11.) _____ you <u>over</u>, but I'm afraid I'll be away for the holidays ... but maybe in January. Any weekend would be OK. (12.) _____ your <u>pick</u>.

ALYSSA: That's when we go to the country.

LAURA: Well, whenever.

▶ FOR AN EXTRA CHALLENGE: Do both His Point of View and Her Point of View.

▶ GETTING IT RIGHT

8. **Where Do You Put "It"?**   Read each sentence. If the pronoun object is in the right position, mark *OK*. If the pronoun object is in the wrong position, write in the correct phrase. Compare answers with a partner and try to agree.

1. My father hates this old car. I don't know why he's holding onto <u>it</u>.

   OK [ ]   Correction: _____

2. You must be very close to your sister and brother-in-law. You're always having over <u>them</u>.

   OK [ ]   Correction: _____

3. I love a view of the ocean. I'm so glad our apartment looks out on <u>it</u>.

   OK [ ]   Correction: _____

4. You won't be able to sell the house until you get some work done. You've got to fix up <u>it</u>.

   OK [ ]   Correction: _____

5. I just love my new apartment. I can't wait to move into <u>it</u>.

   OK [ ]   Correction: _____

6. After you finish washing the car, you should clean <u>it</u> out.

   OK [ ]   Correction: _____

7. This is such a beautiful dress. I hate to pass up <u>it</u>.

   OK [ ]   Correction: _____

LISTEN IN

9. Listen and Answer   Listen to each commercial on the radio. Mark the answer that applies to that commercial.

Commercial 1

1. Who is this commercial speaking to?

    a. [ ] People who are trying to sell their current apartment
    b. [ ] People who want to buy a house in the country
    c. [ ] People who live in a small apartment without a view

2. Which apartments are available through Abigail Realty? (*Mark two answers.*)

    a. [ ] Apartments with a good view of the city
    b. [ ] Apartments that are in good condition
    c. [ ] Apartments that are in a different city

Commercial 2

3. What does this commercial advise people to do?

    a. [ ] Keep the house they're currently living in because it's not a good time to sell
    b. [ ] Not keep the house they're currently living in if they're not happy with it
    c. [ ] Leave their current job and work for Suburban Realty

4. What does Suburban Realty sell? (*Mark two answers.*)

    a. [ ] Small houses that don't require a lot of work
    b. [ ] Large houses that are big enough for entertaining guests
    c. [ ] Large apartments that have everything you've ever wanted

5. What does Suburban Realty invite clients to do?

    a. [ ] Choose homes over the phone because there aren't many available
    b. [ ] Visit the office and choose from a large selection of houses
    c. [ ] Move to new apartments

Commercial 3

6. Who is the residence for?

    a. [ ] It's for people in their thirties who like to move frequently.
    b. [ ] It's for older people who have trouble going from place to place.
    c. [ ] It's for people younger than sixty who don't like to cook their own meals.

7. What does the commercial encourage people to do?

    a. [ ] Think about living at the residence
    b. [ ] Be more active
    c. [ ] Become a staff member at the residence

8. What are some of the jobs the staff members do for residents? (*Mark two answers.*)

    a. [ ] Help residents move and drive them to restaurants for dinner
    b. [ ] Keep the garden in good condition and bring meals to the rooms
    c. [ ] Help residents with their chores when they're too tired to do them themselves

Commercial 4

9. Who is this commercial speaking to?

    a. [ ] Those who already have a few children
    b. [ ] Those who want to have children and need more space
    c. [ ] Those who like to eat all their meals in restaurants

10. What will you be able to do in the apartments from this realtor?

    a. [ ] Eat meals at home
    b. [ ] Sleep better and have better dreams
    c. [ ] Become a decorator

11. What does the commercial advise?

    a. [ ] Don't wait until the prices increase and you can't afford one of these
       apartments.
    b. [ ] Don't eat in the kitchen.
    c. [ ] Don't miss the chance to get free decorating advice when you buy an
       apartment.

Compare answers with a partner and try to agree. If you need to, look at the Tapescript
on pages 175–176.

SPEAK UP

10. **Let's Get Personal**   Is this you? For each statement, circle *True* or *False*. Share your
    answers in a small group. Are the other students in your group just like you?

    1. It's easy for me to get around town.   True   False

    2. I love to fix up my home.   True   False

    3. I would rather go to a restaurant than eat in.   True   False

    4. I feel a little cooped up in my apartment (or house or dormitory).   True   False

    5. I usually stay up past midnight.   True   False

    6. I can never pass up a bargain[2].   True   False

    7. I would like to move out of my current home.   True   False

    8. I hate to clean out the drawers in my bedroom.   True   False

    9. I love to have friends over.   True   False

    10. I usually hold onto things even if I don't use them anymore.   True   False

 FOR AN EXTRA CHALLENGE: After sharing your answers, go back and circle the idiom in
each sentence. Check your answers in the Answer Key on page 186.

---

[2] *bargain*: something you can buy at a good price

11. Act It Out: Buying or Renting a Home

Read the ads below. Find two or three homes that you're interested in. Then prepare questions to ask a real estate agent, using as many idioms as you can from the list on pages 45–46. Then, take turns acting out the conversations with your partner.

SAMPLE QUESTIONS FOR ADVERTISEMENT 1:

The ad says the house has a large kitchen. Is that an **eat-in** kitchen?

It also says it has a great view. What does the house **look out on**?

1.

4-bedroom modern house in quiet Riverside. Large kitchen, great view, separate guest house. Needs some work. Reasonable. Robin Wallace, 555–1999

2.

Custom-built modern house offers 3 bedrooms, 2 baths, living room with fireplace, playroom. Mother-in-law apartment over 3-car garage. Pretty good condition. Walk to train. Hassan Real Estate, 555–8000

3.

1-bedroom apt., tiny guest room and eat-in kitchen in safe, convenient area. Doorman building. Walk to midtown. Many restaurants nearby. Available immediately. Act now. Barker Rentals, 555–7766

4.

Why rent when you can own a home in Princeton? Close to university. Small yard, easy maintenance. Priced for quick sale. Hill Realty, 555–5454

5.

Golf course view. This distinctive home in the elegant Country Club section is only 20 minutes from the heart of town. Call our office today. Dover Realtors, 555–8000

6.

Large 2-bedroom apartment, 35th floor. Great views. Conveniently located, center of town. Recently renovated. Park Avenue Realty, 555–4540

12. **Write a Composition**   Using as many idioms as you can from the list on pages 45–46, write an essay about one of the topics below. In a small group, read your essay. Get feedback on your writing and revise your work.

   a. Write about the topic "What I Like (or Dislike) About My Home."

   b.   Look at the pictures below. Choose the home you would like to move into. Write about why you chose that home.

13. Review the Idioms   With a partner, decide which of the activities below will help you learn the most.

- Write the meaning of each idiom.

- Write a sample sentence for each idiom.

- Give examples of subjects and/or objects that go with each idiom. (Note: Not all idioms require objects.)

  EXAMPLE: <u>This class</u> has almost wrapped up <u>this chapter</u>.
  $\quad\quad\quad\quad\quad$ S $\quad\quad\quad\quad\quad\quad\quad\quad\quad\quad\quad\quad\quad$ O

- Practice saying the idioms with correct stress. (Verbs and adverbs/particles are stressed, but the verbs *to be* and *to have* and one-syllable prepositions are not stressed.) If possible, practice saying the idioms in sentences.

Then use the list that follows to help you complete the activities together. Note the two symbols for objects.

> ( ) = The object of the preposition. It goes after the preposition.
>
> [ ] = The object of the phrasal verb. If it is a pronoun, it goes between the verb and adverb/particle. If it is a noun, it can go between the verb and the adverb/particle *or* after the adverb/particle.

1. clean [ ] out _____

_____

2. coop up; coop up in ( ) _____

_____
Usage: Informal; often passive: *He was cooped up all day.*

3. eat in _____

_____
Usage: Often used as adjective: *an eat-in kitchen*

4. eat out _____

_____

5. fix [ ] up _____

_____
Usage: Informal

6. get around; get around town _____

_____

7. have [ ] over _____

_____

8. hold onto ( ) _____

_____

9. keep [ ] up _____

_____
Usage: Informal; noun: *upkeep*

10. look out on ( ) _____

_____

11. make room for ( ) _____

_____

12. move in; move into ( ) _____

_____

13. move out; move out of ( ) _____

_____

14. pass [ ] up _____

_____

15. stay up _____

_____

16. take one's pick _____

_____

Chapter 4 CRIME

GETTING STARTED

1. Answer the Survey   Write your answers to the following survey questions on crime. Then interview a partner and write his or her answers. Discuss your answers.

> At the end of the twentieth century, there were almost 2 million people held in prisons or jails in the United States. This prison population is the largest in the world.

My answers	My partner's answers
1. Do you think the United States has more violent crime than other countries? [ ] Yes. [ ] No.	1. Do you think the United States has more violent crime than other countries? [ ] Yes. [ ] No.
2. Do you think there is too much violence on television and in movies in the U.S.? [ ] Yes. [ ] No.	2. Do you think there is too much violence on television and in movies in the U.S.? [ ] Yes. [ ] No.
3. Check the three best ways of preventing violent crime: [ ] stricter gun control (who can buy a gun, how often one can buy guns, etc.) [ ] longer prison sentences (time spent in prison) [ ] the death penalty[1] [ ] community programs to help young people who are getting in trouble [ ] more police [ ] more jobs [ ] citizens protecting their own neighborhoods	3. Check the three best ways of preventing violent crime: [ ] stricter gun control (who can buy a gun, how often one can buy guns, etc.) [ ] longer prison sentences (time spent in prison) [ ] the death penalty[1] [ ] community programs to help young people who are getting in trouble [ ] more police [ ] more jobs [ ] citizens protecting their own neighborhoods

[1] *the death penalty:* also called *capital punishment*; includes death by lethal injection or gas, electrocution, hanging, or the firing squad; legal in the United States, but not used in all states

INTRODUCTION OF IDIOMS

2. Read Between the Lines   Read the summary of the novel *In Cold Blood*. This novel, by Truman Capote, was based on a true story. With a partner, try to understand what it says. Then do Exercise 3.

Gunned Down

In November, 1959, Herbert Clutter, a Midwestern farmer, decided to buy a forty-thousand-dollar life insurance policy. He wanted to be sure his family would have enough money if something happened to him and he died unexpectedly. He signed the insurance policy on Friday the thirteenth. Tragically and ironically, the next day, Mr. Clutter, his wife Bonnie, and two of their children, Kenyon and Nancy, were all **gunned down**.

It happened in the town of Holcomb, Kansas, population 270. Two ex-convicts, Dick Hickock and Perry Smith, had come to the Clutter farmhouse in the middle of the wheat fields, looking for money. Dick had heard about the Clutters from another prisoner, Floyd Wells, when they were both **doing time** at Kansas State Penitentiary in Lansing. Wells had worked for a year at the Clutter farm and said that Mr. Clutter kept ten thousand dollars in a safe in his house. When Dick got out of jail, he decided to rob the Clutters' safe and leave no witnesses. And he knew who would help him, his friend Perry Smith. When they **broke in**, they found four members of the Clutter family at home. Things quickly **got out of hand**. They **tied** the family **up** and then killed each one in cold blood.[2] Dick and Perry **made off with** the grand sum of forty dollars.

After the crime, Dick and Perry **hid out in** Mexico but soon returned to the United States. Dick was sure they would **get away with** their crime, but Perry feared they would be caught as they both had been before. The only clues were footprints in blood, and the only witness was Floyd Wells, Dick's cellmate. Agents from the Kansas Bureau of Investigation used these leads to **track down** the killers, who **were on the run** for six weeks. At the end of December, Dick and Perry were **picked up** in Las Vegas, Nevada. They were taken to Kansas, where they were **locked up**.

Perry confessed to killing Mr. Clutter and his son but accused Dick of shooting Mrs. Clutter and her daughter. Dick, however, never **owned up to** the killings. Instead, he **put the blame on** Perry. When the case **went to trial**, both men were convicted of murder in the first degree. Capital punishment was legal in Kansas at that time, and both of them were given the death penalty. They were scheduled to die on Friday, May 13th, 1960.

While they **were behind bars** on death row, Dick and Perry hoped to get their sentence reduced to life in prison. Dick kept writing letters to legal organizations saying that they hadn't been given a fair trial because the judge and many of the jurors had been friends of the Clutter family. In this way, they managed to delay their execution for five years. But on April 14th, 1965, they climbed the thirteen steps to the gallows and were hanged by the neck until dead.

*   *   *

The country learned of the multiple murder because the author Truman Capote went to Kansas to write an article about it for *The New Yorker* magazine. Capote eventually turned his article into the book *In Cold Blood: A True Account of a Multiple Murder and Its Consequences. In Cold Blood* was called a "nonfiction novel," because it was suspenseful and moving like a work of fiction. However, it was based on the author's observations and interviews as well as official records of the investigation, trial, and execution of the murderers. It became a bestseller.

---

2 *in cold blood:* without any emotion

3. Line by Line   With a partner, mark the answer that explains the summary of the novel on page 48. Then look at the summary and find the sentence with the same meaning. Write that sentence below.

1. What happened to the Clutter family the day after Herbert Clutter bought life insurance?

   a. [ ] They bought guns to protect themselves.
   b. [ ] Two of the children killed their parents.
   c. [ ] Four of them were shot to death.
   Sentence: _____

2. What did Dick and Perry do to the Clutter family?

   a. [ ] They broke their backs and then killed them.
   b. [ ] They shook hands with them.
   c. [ ] They used rope to stop them from leaving and then killed them.
   Sentence: _____

3. What did Dick and Perry do after their crimes at the Clutter house?

   a. [ ] They went to the police and confessed to their crimes.
   b. [ ] They escaped with the money they had stolen.
   c. [ ] They put the money they had stolen in a secret place in Mexico.
   Sentence: _____

4. What did they do for six weeks?

   a. [ ] They ran in a race in the United States.
   b. [ ] They stayed in the United States.
   c. [ ] They moved around and hid in different places.
   Sentence: _____

5. What happened to them in Las Vegas?

   a. [ ] They were caught and taken away by the detectives.
   b. [ ] They were questioned and released by the detectives.
   c. [ ] They were killed by the detectives.
   Sentence: _____

6. What did Dick say about his role in the murders?

   a. [ ] He admitted that he killed two of the Clutters.
   b. [ ] He didn't admit to killing anyone.
   c. [ ] He said it was his gun, but he hadn't used it.
   Sentence: _____

GLOBAL VILLAGE TORONTO
(The Language Workshop)
180 Bloor Street West, Suite 202
Toronto, Ontario
M5S 2V6 Canada

Crime   49

7. According to Dick, who was responsible for the murders?

    a. [ ] Dick said he was responsible for killing Mrs. Clutter and her daughter.

    b. [ ] Dick said Perry killed Mr. Clutter and his son.

    c. [ ] Dick said Perry was responsible for killing the four Clutters.

    Sentence: _____

4. **Match It Up**   Read each line of a conversation between two detectives, Carol Hare and Daniel Viera. They're discussing the Clutter murders. Carol is sharing her thoughts on the murders. Daniel doesn't say much; he mostly paraphrases what Carol says and gives support. With a partner, write the letter of each of Daniel's responses next to Carol's lines.

DETECTIVE CAROL HARE

____ 1. I bet the killers have **done time** before. They're not new to crime.

____ 2. It's strange that they **broke in** while the family was home.

____ 3. Maybe they didn't know the family members were there, but when they saw them, the situation **got out of hand**.

____ 4. They must have thought they would **make off with** a bundle of money.

____ 5. All I can say is I hope we can **track** them **down** and **lock** them **up** before they kill somebody else.

____ 6. And I want to be there when the case **goes to trial**.

____ 7. It would really be too bad if they **got away with** it.

____ 8. They should **be behind bars** for the rest of their lives.

DETECTIVE DANIEL VIERA

a. Yes, it would be terrible if they were never punished for their crimes.

b. I want to find them as soon as possible, too, and put them right in jail.

c. I agree. They've probably been in jail a couple of times.

d. Yes, when the killers saw those four people, things probably became worse quickly.

e. It *is* unusual that they forced their way into the house when four people were there.

f. I agree. They should remain in prison until they die.

g. Yeah, but they didn't steal much.

h. Me too. I want to be in the room when the case is presented in court.

5. Figure It Out   Mark the answer that is closest in meaning to each idiom. Compare answers with a partner and try to agree.

SITUATION 1: A husband and wife reading the newspaper at breakfast

1. Peggy: Look at this. There was a robbery at Standard Bank yesterday. Two guys **made off with** 144,000 dollars.

   a. [ ] were arrested with   b. [ ] deposited   c. [ ] stole and left with

2. Gerard: I wonder if they'll **get away with** it.

   a. [ ] leave the country with   b. [ ] not be punished for   c. [ ] hide

SITUATION II: A television news report

3. Newscaster: Another off-duty police officer was **gunned down** this morning.

   a. [ ] killed by accident   b. [ ] killed with a gun   c. [ ] injured

4. Newscaster: It happened when the officer tried to stop a fight on a train. The situation quickly **got out of hand**, and someone shot him.

   a. [ ] became uncontrollable   b. [ ] became a little tense   c. [ ] improved

SITUATION III: Two students on a college campus

5. Brenda: We can relax. The detectives finally **tracked down** that serial killer.

   a. [ ] put in jail for a long time   b. [ ] looked for but didn't find
   c. [ ] found after a search

6. Vera: Oh really? I heard he was **hiding out** somewhere in Gainesville, Florida. I'm glad they caught him.

   a. [ ] staying in a secret place   b. [ ] killing more people
   c. [ ] living on the street

SITUATION IV: Two co-workers in an office

7. Ronald: Sandra's apartment was **broken into** last night.

   a. [ ] destroyed   b. [ ] investigated illegally   c. [ ] entered illegally

8. Alyssa: She told me. She said the police **locked up** an eighteen-year-old who was found with her stereo in his car.

   a. [ ] questioned   b. [ ] put in jail   c. [ ] searched for

9. Radio Announcer: The FBI—Federal Bureau of Investigation—just **picked up** a revolutionary from the 1970s.

    a. [ ] questioned   b. [ ] searched for   c. [ ] caught

10. Driver: I can't believes she's **been on the run** since then.

    a. [ ] hiding and moving from place to place
    b. [ ] competing in races
    c. [ ] trying to get caught by the police

6. Match the Pictures and Sentences
With a partner, match each sentence with one of the pictures below. Then read the story to your partner in the correct order.

___ 1.   a. The case is **going to trial** this week.

___ 2.   b. When they were caught, neither **owned up** to the crime. They **put the blame on** each other.

___ 3.

___ 4.   c. Two young men **tied up** a bank clerk and **made off with** 15,000 dollars.

    d. Because they're so young, they probably won't **do** much **time**.

 FOR AN EXTRA CHALLENGE: Cover the sentences and tell your partner the story again. Remember to use crime idioms.

7. Game: Do the Right Thing   You and your partner are police officers in a neighborhood with a lot of crime. People who live in the neighborhood come to you for help. They tell you that some teenagers have broken into an empty building and are using drugs and selling them in the building. This brings dangerous people with guns into the area. As a result, recently there have been shootings, fights, and burglaries in the neighborhood. The situation is getting out of hand. They want to know what you will do.

With your partner, read and discuss all the responses below. Then choose one. To find out the results of your choice (and your score), check the Answer Key on pages 187–188. Share your score with the class. Then tell another pair of students what you did about the drug dealers and what happened to you as a result. Use the idioms from this chapter.

Responses

1. Go to the building, **track down** the drug dealers, and **gun** them **down**.

2. Talk to the drug dealers and tell them they must **own up to** selling drugs and stop doing it right away or you will **lock** them **up**.

3. **Hide out in** the building and make a videotape of the group taking and selling drugs. Then catch them and **lock** them **up**. Let a judge decide how long they should **be behind bars**.

4. **Pick up** the drug dealers and give them a choice: They can be **locked up** or sent to a program to help drug addicts.

5. **Hide out in** the building and catch the drug dealers. Then **tie** them **up** and lead them into the middle of the street. Let the people in the neighborhood decide what to do with them.

6. Get the names and addresses of the drug dealers, **track down** their parents, and **put the blame on** them. Then **pick up** the parents for letting their children **get away with** using and selling drugs. Make the parents **do time**.

8. It's News to Me   Read each example of authentic language taken from newspapers and magazines and try to notice the idioms. With a partner, discuss the meaning of each idiom in that particular context. Write the idiom and its meaning below. (*Excerpt 3 has two idioms.*)

1. A headline in *The New York Times*

> ## 2 YOUTHS IN COLORADO SCHOOL SAID TO GUN DOWN AS MANY AS 23 AND KILL THEMSELVES IN A SIEGE

_____ = _____

2. An excerpt from the Week in Review section of *The New York Times*

Less Crime, More Criminals

BY TIMOTHY EGAN

Americans do not use more drugs, on average, than people in other nations; but the United States . . . has chosen a path of incarceration for drug offenders. More than 400,000 people are behind bars for drug crimes—and nearly a third of them are locked up for simply possessing an illicit drug . . .

_____ = _____

3. An excerpt from *The New York Times* Book Review

Yankees in the Belfry

A Review of *My First Cousin Once Removed: Money, Madness, and the Family of Robert Lowell*, By Sarah Payne Stuart

By Reeve Lindbergh

Robert Lowell, known to his family and friends as Bobby, was a manic-depressive as well as a poet. He also had a tendency to drink heavily, to write about his family in a way that upset them, and to leave his wives. "Bobby had created a lot of turmoil in the family before I was born," his younger cousin Sarah writes, "but then he had won the Pulitzer Prize and the National Book Award, and for years he could get away with anything."

_____ = _____

9. Where Do You Put "It"?   Read each sentence. If the pronoun object is in the right position, mark *OK*. If the pronoun object is in the wrong position, write in the correct phrase. Compare answers with a partner and try to agree.

1. The hijackers took two passengers on the plane and tied <u>them</u> up.

    OK [ ]   Correction: _____

2. The leader of the gang gunned down <u>him</u>.

    OK [ ]   Correction: _____

3. When they realized how much money was in the safe, the robbers decided to break <u>it</u> into.

    OK [ ]   Correction: _____

4. The CIA[3] searched for the assassin in five countries and finally tracked <u>him</u> down in Turkey.

    OK [ ]   Correction: _____

5. Most people in the neighborhood would like the police to catch those drug dealers, lock up <u>them</u>, and throw away the key.

    OK [ ]   Correction: _____

6. After the woman stole the diamond necklace, the police picked <u>her</u> up for speeding and found it accidentally.

    OK [ ]   Correction: _____

---

3 *CIA:* Central Intelligence Agency

10. Listen and Answer The following interviews take place at a police station. Listen to each interview and the question that follows it. Read the three choices below and mark the one that answers the question correctly.

1. a. [ ] Someone broke the lock but didn't get into the apartment.
   b. [ ] Someone entered the woman's apartment illegally and stole some things.
   c. [ ] Someone broke the woman's TV and VCR while she was at the store.

2. a. [ ] Shoot to kill the other man, then stay in a secret place on the roof of the building
   b. [ ] Shoot to scare the other man, then stand outside the building
   c. [ ] Take the gun from the man with the brown paper bag, then put it in a hiding place on the roof of the building

3. a. [ ] Call more witnesses
   b. [ ] Appear in court
   c. [ ] Find the murderer

4. a. [ ] The driver said it was the students' fault, but the club said it was the driver's fault.
   b. [ ] The police blamed the accident on the drugs that were at the party.
   c. [ ] There were too many people at the party, and several students hit each other.

5. a. [ ] He was arrested for robbery before, but he never actually spent time in jail.
   b. [ ] He had always shown good behavior until the robbery.
   c. [ ] He was arrested and went to jail, but he was freed early.

6. a. [ ] If the boys are not punished for what they did
   b. [ ] If the same thing happens again
   c. [ ] If the boys who did this move to another state

7. a. [ ] Visiting relatives in Philadelphia
   b. [ ] Robbing banks in New Jersey
   c. [ ] Moving around and hiding

8. a. [ ] Her husband is going to jail for kidnapping her son.
   b. [ ] She may not have to spend more time in jail if she admits what she did and says why she did it.
   c. [ ] She needs to explain why she locked her son out of the house if she doesn't want to spend more time in jail.

Check your answers in the Answer Key on page 188. For ones you found difficult, read the Tapescript on pages 176–177.

SPEAK UP

11. Information Gap: Communicate and Collaborate   Work with a partner. Student A follows the directions below. At the same time, Student B turns to pages 167–168 of Appendix D and follows the directions there.

Student A's Directions, Part 1

You are a news reporter preparing an article on famous crimes of the twentieth century. One of these crimes was the murder of Nicole Brown Simpson and her friend Ronald Goldman. Nicole Simpson's ex-husband, O. J. Simpson, a famous football player and television sports commentator, was accused of murdering them.

What do you need to know about this case to write your article? The following questions will get you started:

> Why was the case so famous?
> Were the victims **gunned down** or killed in another way?
> Did the case **go to trial**? What happened?

Now, prepare additional questions with these idioms:

own up to	*put the blame on*	*lock up*
do time	*track down*	*be behind bars*

Finally, ask Student B—a law professor and an expert on the case—your questions and take notes on the answers. When you are finished, go to Part 2 below and answer Student B's questions about another famous crime. You will write your article later.

Student A's Directions, Part 2

You are a presidential historian. Student B is a news reporter preparing an article on famous crimes of the twentieth century. Student B will ask you questions about the assassination (murder) of John F. Kennedy, President of the United States.

Read about the case on the next page and use the information to answer Student B's questions. When you are finished, go to Create a News Story on page 58 and write your article about the O. J. Simpson case.

The Assassination of President Kennedy

On November 22, 1963, President John F. Kennedy and the First Lady, Jacqueline Kennedy, traveled to Texas. While the President's motorcade moved through downtown Dallas, friendly crowds cheered the President. But suddenly, as the cars moved through the streets, the President was shot. He was rushed to the hospital, where he died a half-hour later. He was only forty-six years old. Kennedy was the fourth U.S. president to be assassinated. (The others were Abraham Lincoln in 1865, James A. Garfield in 1881, and William McKinley in 1901.) Kennedy's alleged killer, Lee Harvey Oswald, hid out in a book depository and fired his gun from an upper floor of the building near the route of the President's motorcade.

Oswald was tracked down and put in jail for the murder. He was an unstable person who was involved in an organization that supported Fidel Castro of Cuba, and he had spent some time in the former Soviet Union. Oswald would not own up to the crime while he was behind bars. Two days after his arrest, in front of millions of television viewers, Oswald was gunned down by Jack Ruby, the owner of a Dallas nightclub.

The American public had many questions about the assassination. Lyndon Johnson, who had become President, appointed a group to investigate the assassination. It was called the Warren Commission because it was headed by Supreme Court Chief Justice Earl Warren. The commission wanted to know if Oswald was really the killer and if he had acted alone or if others were involved. The investigation concluded that Oswald was the President's assassin and that he had acted alone. But many Americans did not accept the conclusions of the Warren Commission. They felt that there were still too many unanswered questions.

Write It Out

12. **Create a News Story**   Write an article on the crime you asked your partner about: either the Simpson and Goldman murders or the Kennedy assassination. Use the notes you took to draft your article. Use as many idioms as you can from the list on pages 59–60.

13. **Review the Idioms** With a partner, decide which of the activities below will help you learn the most.

- Write the meaning of each idiom.

- Write a sample sentence for each idiom.

- Give examples of subjects and/or objects that go with each idiom. (Note: Not all idioms require objects.)

  EXAMPLE: <u>This class</u> has almost wrapped up <u>this chapter</u>.
             S   O

- Practice saying the idioms with correct stress. (Verbs and adverbs/particles are stressed, but the verbs *to be* and *to have* and one-syllable prepositions are not stressed.) If possible, practice saying the idioms in sentences.

Then use the list that follows to help you complete the activities together. Note the two symbols for objects.

> ( ) = The object of the preposition. It goes after the preposition.
>
> [ ] = The object of the phrasal verb. If it is a pronoun, it goes between the verb and adverb/particle. If it is a noun, it can go between the verb and the adverb/particle *or* after the adverb/particle.

1. be behind bars _____

_____

2. be on the run _____

_____

3. break in; break into ( ) _____

_____

4. do time _____

_____

5. get away with ( ) _____

_____
Usage: Informal; implies the person was guilty

6. get out of hand _____

_____
Usage: Informal

7. go to trial _____

_____

8. gun [ ] down _____

_____

9. hide out in ( ) _____

_____

10. lock [ ] up; lock [ ] up in ( ) _____

_____

Usage: Informal; often passive: *He was locked up.*

11. make off with ( ) _____

_____

12. own up to ( ) _____

_____

13. pick [ ] up _____

_____

Usage: Informal; often passive: *She was picked up quickly.*

14. put the blame on ( ) _____

_____

Usage: also *place the blame on*

15. tie [ ] up _____

_____

16. track [ ] down _____

_____

Chapter 5

LOVE

GETTING STARTED

1. **Share Your Reactions**   In a small group, discuss the following questions about marriage. Share your answers with the class.

"He's very well off.[1] He's got all the quantities I admire."

1. Which of the following are considered important for a successful marriage in your country?

    - romantic love (feelings of affection and passion toward another person)
    - social considerations (the same social class, race, ethnic group, or religion)
    - economic considerations (financial security, earning potential)

2. Most Americans, even today, marry someone from the same social class, that is, someone with a similar economic, occupational, and educational background. (They also marry someone of the same race, religion, and age and think romantic love is important for a successful marriage.) Do you think it's important to marry someone from the same social class? Why or why not?

3. What do *you* think is most important for a successful marriage? Why?

4. What do you think of arranged marriages? Are they common in your country?

---

[1] *well off*: rich

INTRODUCTION OF IDIOMS

2. Read Between the Lines   Read the discussion of the movie *Titanic* by two reviewers. With a partner, try to understand what it says. Then do Exercise 3.

Falling in Love on the Titanic

DEVON: This next film, *Titanic*, just **bowled** me **over**. James Cameron, the director of the science fiction movies *The Terminator* and *Aliens*, has **shifted gears** and made a beautiful, gripping love story.

WOLF: It's gripping only if you're a teenager, Paul.

DEVON: I disagree. I think *Titanic* is the most universally appealing romance since *Gone with the Wind*. Here's a story that follows two young people from very different backgrounds. Jack Dawson, a free spirit, alone in the world, with no money, encounters Rose DeWitt Bukater, a member of Philadelphia's upper class.

WOLF: The dialog is awful, and it's a familiar tale: poor boy meets rich girl.

DEVON: I disagree. Rose's father has left the family nothing but debts. To survive, Rose's mother has arranged for her to marry Cal Hockley, a snob, a pain, a bore, who will one day inherit millions.

WOLF: I've heard it all before, Paul.

DEVON: But the way Rose and Jack **run into** each other is romantic and touching. Feeling trapped by her engagement to Cal and a life that is just a series of parties, Rose decides to throw herself into the sea. Jack goes after her and rescues her from certain suicide.

WOLF: Yes, another rich girl is saved from **doing** herself **in**.

DEVON: But Jack does it so well. He has the delicacy, the imagination, the strength to save her.

WOLF: And what is his reward? Dinner with the family, fiancé, and friends. The scene seemed unnatural to me.

DEVON: But what about that plain-speaking American character Molly Brown? She was amusing at the dinner. She **became fond of** the spirited Jack who managed to **hold** his **own with** that upper-class group.

WOLF: Molly Brown? I didn't believe her. She was a Hollywood device. The wealthy woman who, it **turns out**, wasn't born rich, and of course, had a heart of gold.

DEVON: I found her believable. And the noble meeting of Rose and Jack which leads to their **falling in love**—to me that's possible. Opposites attract. They see in the other person something that's missing in themselves. In a short time, they **are crazy about** each other, and their romance threatens Rose's engagement to Cal.

WOLF: It all **came across as** contrived to me.

DEVON: What about Cal's reaction to the lovers? In the beginning of the film, he **keeps a stiff upper lip**, which is indeed stereotypical. But later, suspecting that Rose has **fallen for** Jack, he sends his servant to **keep an eye on** the pair. When he learns that they've been **fooling around** below deck, he explodes with rage. And then,

when he discovers Jack's sketch of Rose wearing nothing but the blue diamond, it ⊣
drives him **crazy**. Cal actually tries to kill Jack when the ship is sinking.

WOLF: I wouldn't blame him. Of course, the sinking is very dramatic. But a sinking ship always is, and so is the possibility of death. An easy device.

DEVON: I think you've grown cynical like Cal.

WOLF: I feel lucky to have survived the latest disaster film.

▶ UNDERSTANDING THE MEANING

3. Line by Line   With a partner, mark the answer that explains the movie review on pages 62–63. Then look at the movie review and find the sentence with the same meaning. Write that sentence below.

1. What is Devon's reaction to the movie *Titanic*?

   a. [ ] He doesn't like it at all.
   b. [ ] He likes it very much.
   c. [ ] He likes it a little.
   Sentence: _____

2. How do Rose and Jack meet on the ship?

   a. [ ] They are running on the ship when they meet.
   b. [ ] They plan to meet before her suicide.
   c. [ ] They meet accidentally when she is about to jump from the ship.
   Sentence: _____

3. What is Molly Brown's reaction to Jack?

   a. [ ] She is scandalized by him.
   b. [ ] She grows to like him.
   c. [ ] She doesn't really like him.
   Sentence: _____

4. At the dinner table, how does Jack communicate with the first-class passengers?

   a. [ ] He is embarrassed and can't speak.
   b. [ ] He doesn't know what to say to such rich people.
   c. [ ] He speaks well and people listen to him.
   Sentence: _____

5. What happens to Jack and Rose after they meet?

   a. [ ] Rose and Jack begin to love each other.
   b. [ ] Jack loves Rose, but she doesn't love him.
   c. [ ] Rose loves Jack, but he doesn't love her.
   Sentence: _____

6. How do Jack and Rose feel about each other a little later?

a. [ ] They don't like each other as much as they did in the beginning.

b. [∨] They love each other very much.

c. [ ] Each one thinks the other is insane.

Sentence: _____

7. How does Cal react to Rose's behavior in the beginning of the movie?

a. [∨] He doesn't show his emotions at all.

b. [ ] He shows his emotions and gets very upset.

c. [ ] He doesn't care what she does as long as she marries him.

Sentence: _____ keep an upper lip _____ stiff _____

8. What is Cal's reaction to Jack's sketch of Rose?

a. [∨] He becomes very upset about it.

b. [ ] He thinks it's beautiful.

c. [ ] He doesn't think the art is very good.

Sentence: _____ drive him crazy _____

4. **Match It Up** Read each line of a conversation between two friends, Tanya and Jeff. Tanya is telling Jeff about her reaction to the movie *Titanic*. Jeff doesn't say much; he mostly paraphrases what Tanya says and gives support. With a partner, write the letter of each of Jeff's responses next to Tanya's lines.

TANYA

_c_ 1. I couldn't believe that Rose—who had such a good life—was going to **do** herself **in**.

_b_ 2. I liked Molly Brown. She was rich like the others, but it **turned out** that she hadn't been born rich.

_a_ 3. I also liked Cal. At first, he **came across as** a sophisticated person.

_e_ 4. But he changed when he thought Rose had **fallen for** Jack.

_g_ 5. I loved it when he sent his servant to **keep an eye on** Rose and Jack.

_d_ 6. He really got angry when he heard that Rose and Jack were **fooling around** below deck.

_f_ 7. The director James Cameron certainly **shifted gears** when he made this movie.

JEFF

a. Yes, he certainly appeared to be a refined man in the beginning.

b. Yes, we knew she was different. Only later, it was revealed that she hadn't always been rich.

c. You're right. She didn't seem to have any reason to try to kill herself.

d. He *did* change when he realized Rose was really fascinated by Jack.

e. Oh, that's right. After he was told that his fiancée and Jack were kissing and hugging, he *was* very upset.

f. Yes, he made a big change in this movie.

g. I liked when he told his servant to follow and watch Rose.

5. Choose the Right Card With a partner, choose a greeting card for each situation below.

a. I'm glad everything turned out so well...

b. I think I've fallen in love...

c. It's hard for me to say it, but I'm really fond of you...

d. Your silence is driving me crazy...

___C___ 1. Megan is dating Jim, a student at the same college. After about five dates, she realized that she liked Jim a lot. Megan doesn't show her feelings very easily, so she sent him this card to express how she feels.

_____ 2. Flora arranged a blind date[2] for her best friend Matilda. Matilda really didn't want to go on the date, but she finally agreed. The next day, she called Flora and said she had a great time and liked the guy. Flora sent her this card.

_____ 3. Tanya and Alex have known each other for two years. Last night, they finally went on a date and they both had a fantastic time. To express his deep feelings for Tanya, Alex sent her this card the next day.

_____ 4. Harvey and Rachel have been dating for about two years. Recently, they had a big fight, and Rachel won't return Harvey's phone calls. Harvey sent her this card.

FOR AN EXTRA CHALLENGE: After the matching activity, on a separate piece of paper write a personal note for the inside of each card. Use idioms from this chapter. Then read your notes to the class.

---

[2] *blind date*: a date between two people who have not met before

6. **Figure It Out**   Mark the answer that is closest in meaning to each idiom. Compare answers with a partner and try to agree.

SITUATION I: Two friends discussing a new acquaintance

1. Linda: Gerry was certainly able to **hold** his **own** with that group of lawyers yesterday.

    a. [ ] stop talking   b. [ ] speak loudly   c. [ ] speak well

2. Janice: Yes, he **came across as** a very intelligent and articulate person.

    a. [ ] was seen as   b. [ ] pretended to be   c. [ ] hoped to be seen as

SITUATION II: Two mothers discussing a friend's daughter

3. Elizabeth: I **ran into** Tina's daughter yesterday. What a sweetheart!

    a. [ ] had an appointment with   b. [ ] went jogging with
    c. [ ] unexpectedly met

4. Melanie: Yes, I know. My son **is** absolutely **crazy about** her.

    a. [ ] thinks she's strange   b. [ ] loves her very much   c. [ ] is dating her

SITUATION III: Two women discussing a political scandal

5. Dianne: I just don't know how that senator from Montana managed to **keep a stiff upper lip** while all the TV commentators were discussing her extramarital affair.

    a. [ ] remain dignified   b. [ ] smile a lot   c. [ ] be photographed

6. Marty: I read that she was very upset and angry at home, but when she got to the office, she just **shifted gears** and was very professional.

    a. [ ] relaxed   b. [ ] changed her behavior   c. [ ] worked very hard

SITUATION IV: Two women discussing a news story

7. Debbie: Did you hear about that woman in Denver? After being abused by her husband for ten years, she finally **did** him **in**.

    a. [ ] fought back   b. [ ] told the police about him   c. [ ] killed him

8. Chris: I wonder how things will **turn out** for her. She'll probably spend the rest of her life in jail.

    a. [ ] be in the beginning   b. [ ] be in the end   c. [ ] be immediately

SITUATION V: Two friends talking confidentially

9. Lucy: I can't believe you would **fall for** that actor. He must have several girlfriends already, and lots of women are attracted to him.

    a. [ ] be attracted to   b. [ ] look for   c. [ ] date

10. Maria Elena: I'll tell you one thing—when we go to a party, I **keep an eye on** him.

    a. [ ] look the other way   b. [ ] talk only to him   c. [ ] watch him carefully

7. Information Gap: Soap Opera Game   Work with a partner. Student A follows the directions below. At the same time, Student B turns to pages 169–170 of Appendix D and follows the directions there.

Student A's Directions

The chart below and the chart on page 68 represent the characters and events in Episodes 1 and 6 of a soap opera.[3] Ask your partner questions until you have filled in all the blanks in your charts. Then answer your partner's questions. Do not show your charts to your partner. Try to be the first pair in your class to finish.

EXAMPLE QUESTION: Who is Christina Carlucci **fooling around with**?

Student A's Chart—Episode 1

Christina Carlucci	is married to Eduardo.	is fooling around with _____.
Eduardo Estrada	is married to Christina, but thinks she's fooling around with _____.	is crazy about Casilda.
Mrs. Kimberly Pearson	comes across as a controlling person.	wants Casilda to marry _____.
Casilda Pearson	falls for _____.	wants to do Christina in.
Jonathan Waters	drives Casilda crazy.	runs into _____.
Jessica Trumbull	is still crazy about _____.	meets with Mrs. Pearson.
Private Investigator Brandon Johnson	is hired by Eduardo to keep an eye on _____.	is bowled over by Christina.
Dr. Nicholas Cotton	comes across as a family man.	turns out to be a _____.

---

[3] *soap opera*: a television drama series based on personal relationships and romance

Christina Carlucci	divorces Eduardo.	runs into _____ and falls in love with him while having dinner with Dr. Cotton.
Eduardo Estrada	divorces Christina.	discovers that Casilda has fallen for someone else and tries to do _____ in.
Mrs. Kimberly Pearson	bowls _____ over with the news that Casilda is adopted and can't inherit her millions.	fell for Jonathan years ago.
Casilda Pearson	finds that Dr. Cotton has changed and she is no longer crazy about him.	decides she wants to fool around with _____ _____.
Jonathan Waters	shifts gears and decides _____ doesn't want to be involved with any more women.	drives Christina and Casilda crazy.
Jessica Trumbull	kept a stiff upper lip while Jonathan was fooling around.	tries to do _____ in when she realizes he doesn't want to be with her anymore.
Private Investigator Brandon Johnson	comes across as professional.	proposes to _____ _____.
Dr. Nicholas Cotton	has been keeping an eye on Casilda for his partner.	hopes that _____ will fall in love with the son of his rich partner.

▶ **FOR AN EXTRA CHALLENGE:** With your partner, write a summary of the two episodes. Use the details in the charts and add some details of your own. Share your summary with the class.

8. Where Do You Put "It"?   Read each sentence. If the pronoun object is in the right position, mark *OK.* If the pronoun object is in the wrong position, write in the correct phrase. Compare answers with a partner and try to agree.

1. Her briefcase disappeared at the restaurant. She had forgotten to keep an eye on <u>it</u>.

   OK [ ]   Correction: _____

2. By the end of the movie, the policewoman was dead. The bad guys had done <u>her</u> in.

   OK [ ]   Correction: _____

3. Anita is horrible. Nobody understands why Marco fell <u>her</u> for.

   OK [ ]   Correction: _____

4. I can't believe you ran <u>him</u> into at the supermarket.

   OK [ ]   Correction: _____

5. After the accident, Sara was home for a month. She said her parents drove <u>her</u> crazy.

   OK [ ]   Correction: _____

LISTEN IN

9. Listen, Take Notes, and Answer   Listen to the movie review presented on television and take notes. Then answer the questions.

1. What is the reviewer's opinion of the film *Moonstruck*?
   a. [ ] She hates this movie.
   b. [ ] She likes this movie a lot.
   c. [ ] She's doesn't like it as much as opera.

2. How does Johnny present himself?
   a. [ ] As a Brooklyn boy
   b. [ ] As a bookkeeper who will remain a bachelor
   c. [ ] As a boring man who will remain a bachelor

3. How has the accident affected Ronny?
   a. [ ] It hasn't bothered him at all.
   b. [ ] It has made him very upset.
   c. [ ] It has made him angry because he can't drive.

4. What do we know about the young woman who works with Ronny?
   a. [ ] She doesn't love him.
   b. [ ] She drives him wherever he needs to go.
   c. [ ] She watches him because she loves him.

5. What does Ronny tell Loretta after the night at his apartment?

  a. [ ] That he wants her to marry his brother
  b. [ ] That they can never see each other again
  c. [ ] That he loves her

6. How does Ronny feel about the opera *La Boheme*?

  a. [ ] He likes it very much.
  b. [ ] It's not his favorite opera.
  c. [ ] He hates it.

7. What is Ronny's reaction to Loretta when he sees her at the opera?

  a. [ ] He prefers how she looked before.
  b. [ ] He's amazed at her beauty.
  c. [ ] He thinks she looks OK.

8. What happens when Loretta goes to the opera with Ronny?

  a. [ ] They don't have a good time.
  b. [ ] They meet Loretta's mother and a professor.
  c. [ ] They unexpectedly meet her father and his girlfriend.

9. What does Mrs. Castorini ask the professor?

  a. [ ] Why men are such fools when they're with women
  b. [ ] Why men have relations they shouldn't have with women
  c. [ ] Why men do all the talking

10. What happens at the end of the movie?

  a. [ ] Johnny breaks his engagement, and Loretta gets angry, but the story ends happily.
  b. [ ] Loretta and Johnny are going to start a family after the wedding. The story ends happily.
  c. [ ] Johnny dies and Loretta goes to his funeral in a red dress.

Check your answers in the Answer Key on page 190. For ones you found difficult, read the Tapescript on pages 177-178.

10. Reacting to Poetry   Read the poem. With a partner, try to understand what it says. Then use the idioms in the box to explain the meaning of the poem or to give your reaction to the poem. Read your reactions to the class.

be crazy about	*come across as*	*shift gears*
bowl over	*fall in love with*	*turn out*

The Elusiveness of Love
by Hutchinson K. Fairman

When I try to write a poem
it is to say I love you

When I search for the proper words
it is their feeling I want to give you

When I try to catch that feeling
I find I'd rather hold you

As I put my arms around you
it is your soul I hope to touch.

11. Act It Out: A Support Group   In groups of 3, act out the conversations. One person presents a problem to the group. The others make suggestions for solving the problem using as many idioms as they can from the list on pages 73-74. Make any changes you find necessary, for example, change *women* to *men*.

Problem 1: Once again, I've fallen for someone who's very different from me. We have different interests, different values, and different backgrounds. Why can't I fall in love with someone similar to me?

Problem 2: I always seem to meet women who come across as very nice people in the beginning, but then they turn out to be very nasty. I don't understand.

Problem 3: I'm fond of classical music, but it drives my husband mad. He's crazy about country music, but I hate it. I just don't know what to do.

12. Create a News Story   Read the newspaper headlines below. Choose the one that interests you. Find a partner who chose the same headline. Together, write a news story that goes with the headline using as many idioms as you can from the list on pages 73–74. Then read your story to the class.

> ## Soap Star Shifts Gears and Becomes Full-time Mom

> ## Husband Driven Crazy by Wife's Career

> ## Children Are Crazy About Public Television's New Show

> ## Star of Romantic Comedy Is Bowled Over by Her First Academy Award

> ## Governor Admits to Falling in Love with Beauty Queen

> ## Public Doesn't Fall for Sexy TV Show

> ## Presidential Candidate Comes Across as Surprisingly Liberal

13. Review the Idioms   With a partner, decide which of the activities below will help you learn the most.

- Write the meaning of each idiom.

- Write a sample sentence for each idiom.

- Give examples of subjects and/or objects that go with each idiom.
  (Note: Not all idioms require objects.)

   EXAMPLE: <u>This class</u> has almost wrapped up <u>this chapter</u>.
               s   *o*

- Practice saying the idioms with correct stress. (Verbs and adverbs/particles are stressed, but the verbs *to be* and *to have* and one-syllable prepositions are not stressed.) If possible, practice saying the idioms in sentences.

Then use the list that follows to help you complete the activities together. Note the two symbols for objects.

> ( ) = The object of the preposition. It goes after the preposition.
>
> [ ] = The object of the phrasal verb. If it is a pronoun, it goes between the verb and adverb/particle. If it is a noun, it can go between the verb and the adverb/particle *or* after the adverb/particle.

1. be fond of ( ); become fond of ( ) _____

   _____

2. be crazy about ( ) _____

   _____

3. bowl [ ] over _____

   _____
   Usage: Informal; often passive: He was bowled over.

4. come across as _____

   _____

5. do [ ] in _____

   _____
   Usage: Informal

6. drive [ ] crazy; drive [ ] mad _____

   _____
   Usage: Informal

7. fall for ( ) _____

_____

Usage: Informal

8. fall in love; fall in love with ( ) _____

_____

9. fool around; fool around with ( ) _____

_____

Usage: Informal

10. hold one's own with ( ) _____

_____

11. keep a stiff upper lip _____

_____

12. keep an eye on ( ) _____

_____

13. run into ( ) _____

_____

Usage: Informal

14. shift gears _____

_____

15. turn out _____

_____

Usage: Informal; examples: *It turned out that she was his sister. She turned out to be his sister.*

Review

CHAPTERS 1–5

1. Contrasting Idioms   Underline the idiom that correctly completes each sentence. Then compare answers with a partner and try to agree.

Frank and his sister Paula really [1. get away with / get along with] each other. Both of them are serious students, and they [2. are fond of / are driving at] sports, too. They both play ice hockey and soccer. With all their practices and games, sometimes their schedule [3. gets around / gets out of hand]. Their parents have been trying to [4. talk it over with / talk them into] dropping one sport, but they don't want to. They say they can [5. take it easy / take their pick] during their vacations.

2. The Right Response   Read each sentence containing an idiom and write the letter of the appropriate response next to it. Then do the same for Part 2.

Part 1

SENTENCES WITH IDIOMS

_____ 1. I've been **cooped up** in a tiny office all day.

_____ 2. You know, I'**m** really **fond of** you.

_____ 3. Do you mind if I **bring up** a sensitive issue?

_____ 4. I don't like it when you **cut** me **off** like that.

_____ 5. I'm sorry if I **came across** as a rude person. I didn't mean to.

RESPONSES

a. I like you, too.

b. Sorry. I won't interrupt you again.

c. You need to get some fresh air and a little exercise.

d. Actually, I thought you were just being direct. I liked it.

e. Not at all. We can discuss anything you want.

Part 2

SENTENCES WITH IDIOMS

___ 1. I like you a lot, but I don't want to **do business with** you.

___ 2. Do you think Rick will have to **do time** for tax evasion?

___ 3. It's raining so hard. Maybe we should **eat in** tonight.

___ 4. This house is great, but it needs a lot of work, and it will cost a fortune to **fix** it **up**.

___ 5. I love living in the city. It's so easy to **get around**. You can walk, take a bus, taxi, or train.

RESPONSES

a. But I told you I wanted to go to the new Italian restaurant. It's just down the block.

b. Yeah, it's probably better to just stay friends and not try to work together.

c. I know what you mean. In the suburbs, you can't go anywhere without a car.

d. What kind of improvements were you thinking of?

e. No, it's his first offense. He'll probably be put on probation.

3. It's News to Me   Read each example of authentic language taken from newspapers and magazines and notice the idioms. With a partner, discuss the meaning of each idiom in that particular context. Write the idiom and its meaning below.

1. A headline in *The New York Times*. The article discusses a new agency that will be given the power to do something about the severe traffic problems and air pollution caused by the expansion of cities in the state of Georgia.

Georgia Setting Up Tough Anti-Sprawl Agency

_____ = _____

2. An excerpt from an article in *The New York Times*. The article discusses a warning by a team of doctors after their review of five deaths following liposuction, a type of cosmetic surgery used to remove body fat from the thighs, waist, or abdomen.

But they also said that like any surgery, liposuction could be dangerous if done incorrectly. They found it worrisome that the procedure had been taken up by many doctors, some with minimal training in the technique, who were eager to cash in on people's desperate desire to look sleek in shorts or a swimsuit.

_____ = _____

3. An excerpt from an article in *The New York Times*. The article discusses the opinion of a judge, Robert Bork, on the impeachment of a president.

> "Imagine the founding fathers," Mr. Bork said. "Having spelled out the duties and powers of the President and the sole method for the President's removal (impeachment and conviction), would they want to see a President brought down by 12 people on a jury?" he asked.

_____ = _____

4. An excerpt from an article in *The New York Times* that appeared under a photo of Monica Lewinsky during the impeachment trial of President Clinton.

> Ms. Lewinsky, 25, hurried past a phalanx of reporters and TV cameras parked outside the Mayflower Hotel since her arrival on Saturday and stepped into a limousine.
>
> Her lawyer, Plato Cacheris, said Ms. Lewinsky wanted to get out of town.
>
> "She's been cooped up in the hotel," Mr. Cacheris said. "She's not able to leave, and she wants to get on with her life."

_____ = _____

5. From "Celebrity Picks," in *People* magazine's Special Anniversary Issue: *People 25 Years*. Famous people (actors, politicians, and others) mention their favorite book, movie, or song.

> My favorite book is *The Prince of Tides*. I was bowled over by Pat Conroy's use of language. I began to dole it out to myself in small portions. I didn't want it to end.

_____ = _____

4. Noticing Details About Phrasal Verbs   Answer the questions by circling the letter of the correct answers. Then compare answers with a partner and try to agree.

1. Which three verbs are often used in the passive voice?

    EXAMPLE: He was **bowled over** by her sense of humor.
    (Note the active voice: Her sense of humor bowled him over.)

    a. lock up   b. have over   c. coop up in   d. gun down

2. Which three verbs are usually used in the imperative?

    EXAMPLE: **Lighten up**, Doris.

    a. take it easy   b. go ahead   c. move out   d. hold on

3. Which three verbs are informal? (The example sentences will help you.)

    EXAMPLE: You're **putting** me **on**.

    a. **Lighten up**, OK?   c. Things **got out of hand**.
    b. They were **fooling around**.   d. The case is **going to trial** soon.

4. Which three verbs take gerunds (the *-ing* form of the verb)?

    EXAMPLE: I can't believe he **got away with** *cheating* his partner.

    a. fix up   b. was fond of   c. own up to   d. talk you into

5. Which three are phrasal verbs (verb + adverb)? Remember, with phrasal verbs, the pronoun object always goes *between* the verb and the adverb. Also, the adverb is stressed.

    EXAMPLE: They **tied** *him* **up**. (They TIED him UP.)

    a. spell out   b. fix up   c. run into   d. track down

6. Which three are prepositional verbs (verb + preposition)? Remember, with prepositional verbs, the object of the preposition always goes after the verb and the preposition. Also, the preposition is unstressed.

    EXAMPLE: They're **betting on** *it*. (They're BETting on it.)

    a. fall for   b. run into   c. pass up   d. hold onto

▶ FOR AN EXTRA CHALLENGE: Write a sentence with one phrasal verb from each question above.

5. Find the Topic   Next to each set of idioms, write the topic with which it is associated. The topics are in the box below. Compare answers with a partner and try to agree.

business	*conversation*	*crime*	*love*	*residence*

1. _____   clean out; fix up; look out on

2. _____   branch out; cash in on; pay off

3. _____   bring up; be at a loss for words; lighten up

4. _____   break in; make off with; own up to

5. _____   be crazy about; bowl over; fool around

6. Find the Idioms   Next to each topic, write the idioms that are often associated with that topic. The idioms are in the box below. Compare answers with a partner and try to agree.

buy out *come on*	*do time* *drive crazy*	*fall for* *make room for*	*move out* *ship out*	*spell out* *track down*

1. business   _____   _____

2. conversation _____   _____

3. crime   _____   _____

4. love   _____   _____

5. residence   _____   _____

7. **What Would *You* Say?**   Work in small groups. Read each situation. What would you say? Use one or more idioms in the box to respond to the situation. One student begins. The next student continues until all the responses build into a story, perhaps even a strange one.

1. In class, you saw a close friend cheating on an exam.

   EXAMPLE RESPONSES

   Student A: You know, I hate to **bring** this **up**, but I saw you cheating on the exam yesterday.

   Student B: I'**m** really **fond of** you, so it's hard to discuss this, but I think you should go to the teacher and **own up to** it.

be fond of	*own up to*
bring up (with)	*put the blame on*
get away with	*spell out*
get out of hand	*stay up*
keep a stiff upper lip	*talk over with*

2. You have heard that an old friend thinks you're in love with his girlfriend/her boyfriend. It's not true.

be at a loss for words	*own up to*
bring up (with)	*put the blame on*
fall in love	*run into*
get out of hand	*talk over with*
have over	*turn out*

3. You have discovered that your business partner is stealing money from the company. What will you tell your partner?

bow out	*make off with*
buy out	*own up to*
do business with	*stay up*
get away with	*talk over with*
keep an eye on	*work out*

8. **Game: Charades**   In a small group, each student silently chooses one (or more) of the idioms below and acts it out for the rest of the group. The others in the group must guess which idiom is being acted out.

be crazy about	*put the blame on*
clean out	*surf the Net*
eat out	*take it easy*
keep an eye on	*talk over with*
make room for	*tie up*

6 DEBATE

GETTING STARTED

1. **Take the Quiz**   What do you already know about consumerism—buying and selling habits—in the United States?

   With a partner, complete the survey. Then check the answers at the bottom of the page. Next, discuss the questions below. Compare consumerism in the United States with consumerism in your country.

CONSUMERISM IN THE UNITED STATES

1. There are more shopping centers than high schools in the United States.
   [ ] True   [ ] False

2. How many hours a week do Americans, on average, spend shopping?
   [ ] 1 hour   [ ] 4 hours
   [ ] 2 hours [ ] 6 hours

3. What percentage of families reported (in 1995) that they had saved in the past year?
   [ ] 35%   [ ] 55%   [ ] 75%   [ ] 95%

4. What percentage of families had an outstanding balance on a credit card after paying their most recent bill (in 1995)?
   [ ] 6%   [ ] 12%   [ ] 24%   [ ] 48%

5. What percentage of the typical American newspaper is advertising?
   [ ] 5%   [ ] 25%   [ ] 65%   [ ] 95%

6. How many hours a day is the television on in the typical home in the United States?
   [ ] 1 hour   [ ] 3 hours   [ ] 5 hours [ ] 7 hours

Source: D. L. Durning and Alan Thein, "American Excess," *Federal Reserve Bulletin.*

1. In your opinion, is consumption a good thing or a bad thing? Why?

2. What are the attitudes toward materialism in your country? Do you agree?

3. What is valued more in your country: spending or saving? Do you agree?

Answers: 1. True   2. 6 hours   3. 55%   4. 48%   5. 65%   6. 7 hours

INTRODUCTION OF IDIOMS

2. Read Between the Lines   Read the debate about consumerism. With a partner, try to understand what it says. Then do Exercise 3.

Are We on the Wrong Track?

MODERATOR: In the 1920s, the United States started to become a "consumer society." With the help of mass production, manufacturers could, for the first time, offer more goods than people typically bought. Corporations and the government used advertising to encourage the public to buy more, and even established consumption goals. Of course, during World War II (1939–45), these goals were **set aside**. But since the war, people in the United States have been shopping rather than saving. Is such consumerism good or bad? Let's see if today's debate can **pin down** what is best for the country. Taking the affirmative position—for consumerism—is Alex Svoboda. Dolores Wilson will take the negative position.

SVOBODA: *(affirmative)* What you call consumerism, I call a free-market economy, which produces goods and services people want. Since the War, our economy has raised our standard of living. In other words, we live more comfortable lives.

WILSON: *(negative)* When we discuss consumerism, we mean valuing material things and constant shopping. What I'd like to **draw** your **attention to** is this: Consumerism poses a danger to what is important in life—family, friendships, neighborhoods, and the environment.

SVOBODA: May I **point out** that our free-market economy has brought cars, dishwashers, microwaves, televisions, VCRs,[1] and computers to most middle-class homes? These consumer items have made our lives more interesting and more comfortable. This economy has also stimulated the development of new drugs and medical technology, making us healthier and helping us live longer.

WILSON: Mass production of consumer goods has also brought the pollution of our air and water, the destruction of our forests, and an increase in cancer rates.

SVOBODA: I'd like to **make the point** that new appliances have made it possible for women to get out of the kitchen and into the workplace.

WILSON: In many cases, it's merely to pay for the latest toasters, toys, and TVs.

SVOBODA: But no one's forcing people to buy new things. Apparently, they *want* to have the latest toasters, toys, and TVs—not only for themselves, but for their kids.

WILSON: Of course! Advertisers are constantly tempting them to buy things they don't need. The statistics on this **back** me **up**.

SVOBODA: Oh, let's not **get hung up on** advertising. People have the freedom to buy what they want. And this same freedom drives innovation at companies like Microsoft, and it creates not only new products but new jobs.

---

[1] *VCRs:* videocassette recorders

WILSON: I **have nothing against** Microsoft, and I don't want to **wrangle over** the free-enterprise system. I do, however, think it's a mistake to make material things the center of our lives. Excessive materialism is something we have to **come to terms with**.

MODERATOR: OK, it's time to **sum up**. We'll start with the arguments *for* consumerism.

SVOBODA: Our consumer society has raised our standard of living, created jobs, brought knowledge, entertainment, and convenience into our homes, improved our health, and lengthened our lives. It **boils down to** this: Consumerism has made our lives better.

WILSON: A society that measures individual worth by the material things a person can afford **is on the wrong track**. We've **lost sight of** what's important in life. Materialism is **wreaking havoc with** what we have traditionally valued: friendships, family ties, and fresh air. We can't afford to see how consumerism **plays out** in the future. We should end the consumer lifestyle now.

MODERATOR: Now let's vote on who won the debate: Alex Svoboda who argued *for* consumerism, or Dolores Wilson who argued *against* it.

UNDERSTANDING THE MEANING

3. **Line by Line**   With a partner, mark the answer that explains the debate on pages 82–83. Then look at the debate and find the sentence with the same meaning. Write that sentence below.

1. What happened to the goals for mass consumption during World War II?

   a. [ ] They stayed the same as before the war.
   b. [ ] They were changed slightly.
   c. [ ] They were temporarily not used.
   Sentence: _____

2. In the debate about consumerism, what does the moderator want the participants to do?

   a. [ ] Talk in general about what is best for the country.
   b. [ ] State specifically what is best for the country.
   c. [ ] Ask questions about consumerism.
   Sentence: _____

3. Dolores Wilson says that advertisers try to get people to buy things they don't need. What does she claim the statistics show?

   a. [ ] They don't say anything about this.
   b. [ ] They show that her statement is not true.
   c. [ ] They show that her statement is true.
   Sentence: _____

4. Alex Svoboda says that people have the freedom to buy what they want. What does he think about discussing advertising?

    a. [ ] He doesn't want to waste time talking about it.

    b. [ ] He doesn't want to discuss advertising over the phone.

    c. [ ] He wants to discuss advertising because he thinks it's important.

    Sentence: _____

5. Dolores Wilson has an opinion about excessive materialism. What is it?

    a. [ ] We should learn to accept it.

    b. [ ] We should encourage it.

    c. [ ] We should recognize this problem and do something about it.

    Sentence: _____

6. How does Dolores Wilson feel about a society that measures individual worth by material things?

    a. [ ] She feels a society like that is going in the right direction.

    b. [ ] She feels a society like that is not going in the right direction.

    c. [ ] She feels a society like that is moving too fast.

    Sentence: _____

7. What is materialism doing to what we have traditionally valued, according to Dolores Wilson?

    a. [ ] It is supporting what we have traditionally valued.

    b. [ ] It is raising questions about what we have traditionally valued.

    c. [ ] It is destroying what we have traditionally valued.

    Sentence: _____

4. Paraphrase the Arguments   Read the arguments against consumerism below. Work with a partner. For each idiom in bold, find the meaning in the box. Write the letter of the idiom next to its meaning.

Arguments Against Consumerism

a. The first thing I'd like to **draw your attention to** is the danger materialism poses to our family, our friends, and our neighborhoods.

b. Some **make the point** that consumer goods have helped women in particular, but I believe many women are working merely to buy more things their families don't need.

c. I **have nothing against** innovative companies, but I think it's a mistake to make their products the center of our lives.

d. I don't want to **wrangle over** the free-enterprise system, but we shouldn't measure individual worth by material possessions.

e. We've **lost sight of** what's important in life.

f. My position **boils down to** this: Consumerism takes time and energy away from what really matters.

g. I can **sum up** my position this way: The consumer lifestyle is wrong, it's damaging, and it doesn't bring happiness.

h. We should end the consumer lifestyle now, and not wait to see how it **plays out** in the future.

____ 1. do not oppose

____ 2. can be reduced to

____ 3. argue about

____ 4. state the main facts

____ 5. forgotten

____ 6. make you notice

____ 7. state, claim

____ 8. develops, changes with time

5. Seeing Similarities   Read each question and mark the answers. Then compare answers with a partner.

1. Which *two* idioms have a negative association?
   a. [ ] back somebody up   b. [ ] wreak havoc with   c. [ ] wrangle over

2. Which *two* idioms are related to a short or brief statement?
   a. [ ] set aside   b. [ ] sum up   c. [ ] boil down to

3. Which *two* idioms mean "make someone notice"?
   a. [ ] point out   b. [ ] wrangle over   c. [ ] draw one's attention to

6. **Figure It Out**   Mark the answer that is closest in meaning to each idiom. Compare answers with a partner and try to agree.

SITUATION I: A couple discusses money.

1. Woman: Let's not **wrangle over** money. It's bad for a relationship.
   a. [ ] fight about   b. [ ] talk about   c. [ ] think about

2. Man: I just want to **make the point** that if you don't save when you're young, you won't have any money when you're old.
   a. [ ] summarize the ideas   b. [ ] state the claim   c. [ ] change my view

SITUATION II: A father and teenage daughter discuss her behavior.

3. Father: Listen, you need to **come to terms with** the fact that you have to be home by 11:00 on weekends.
   a. [ ] recognize and accept   b. [ ] disagree with and fight
   c. [ ] discuss and clarify

4. Daughter: Dad, you're **getting hung up on** small stuff.
   a. [ ] pretending not to know about   b. [ ] thinking too much about
   c. [ ] asking about

SITUATION III: Two executives discuss advertising plans at a meeting.

5. Charles: OK, you've given us several reasons for changing our advertising plan. Why don't you **sum up** now?
   a. [ ] restate the main ideas briefly   b. [ ] repeat everything in full
   c. [ ] listen to our reaction

6. Max: It **boils down to** this: Our ads are too similar to those of our competitors. We need something different, something unique.
   a. [ ] can be written like   b. [ ] can be stated simply like
   c. [ ] can be explained like

SITUATION IV: A sociology professor discusses the topic of dating and marriage.

7. Professor: Next I'd like to **draw** your **attention to** the differences in dating patterns in various cultures.
   a. [ ] help you notice   b. [ ] explain every detail about   c. [ ] review for you

8. Student: In the last class, you asked us to **pin down** the reasons that arranged marriages are still common in some cultures.
   a. [ ] think about   b. [ ] discuss generally   c. [ ] state precisely

9. Diana: The police **are** clearly **on the wrong track** in this investigation, but they won't admit it.

   a. [ ] are investigating the train station   b. [ ] are thinking incorrectly
   c. [ ] are getting too much publicity

10. David: I want to see how this is going to **play out** in the press.

   a. [ ] develop   b. [ ] be criticized   c. [ ] be ignored

11. Sophia: I **have nothing against** Ms. Sanchez personally, I just disagree with some of her decisions about hiring and firing.

   a. [ ] really like   b. [ ] don't understand   c. [ ] have no reason to dislike

12. Evelyn: Well, if you want to complain about the office manager she hired, I'll **back you up**.

   a. [ ] explain something to   b. [ ] support   c. [ ] keep quiet around

13. Ms. Wang: It's not a good idea to **set aside** our hiring policies even if he is the president's son.

   a. [ ] weaken   b. [ ] explain   c. [ ] stop using

14. Mr. Johnson: On the other hand, let's not **lose sight of** the fact that he's going to become the president of the company some day, whether we like it or not.

   a. [ ] think about   b. [ ] forget about   c. [ ] complain about

15. Ms. Cook: In the old days, a strike by the office assistants would **wreak havoc**, but today we would simply bring in replacement workers.

   a. [ ] cause minor problems   b. [ ] cause a big disruption
   c. [ ] last a long time

16. Ms. Laramie: Let me **point out** it's not going to be easy to manage workers who don't know what they're doing.

   a. [ ] try to convince you   b. [ ] highlight the fact   c. [ ] quit because

7. Choose the Right Card   With a partner, choose a greeting card for each situation below.

a.

Let's not wrangle over the little things . . .

b.

Let's not lose sight of all the things we enjoyed together. . .

c.

I'll back you up. It's a promise.

d.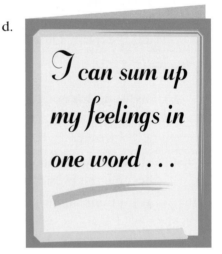

I can sum up my feelings in one word . . .

___ 1. George and Susan have been married for ten years, but they've been fighting a lot lately, and have decided on a trial separation. After living alone for a while, George now feels that they've shared a lot and shouldn't end their marriage. He sends Susan this card.

___ 2. Carla and Kevin are planning their wedding, but they have been fighting about it lately. Kevin wants to wear a tuxedo, but Carla says that's not right for an afternoon wedding. Kevin sends her this card.

___ 3. Recently, Tina and Phil had a fight because Phil decided to change jobs, and Tina wasn't happy with his decision. But now, she thinks it's OK and she wants to tell him that she supports him. She sends him this card.

___ 4. Sal is in love with Hillary. He has told her the things he likes about her, but now he would like to send her a card that says it all briefly. He sends her this card.

▶ FOR AN EXTRA CHALLENGE: After the matching activity, on a separate piece of paper write a personal note for the inside of each card. Use idioms from this chapter. Read your notes to the class.

8. Fill In the Missing Words   Read the letter to the editor. With a partner, write the missing word in each idiom.

To the Editor,

   As your article of September 27th (1.) <u>points</u>_____, many Americans (2.) <u>have something</u>_____ bilingual education programs in public schools. This became obvious in 1998 when Californians voted to end bilingual programs in their state and replace them with one-year immersion classes in English. However, the article failed to (3.) _____ <u>the point</u> that there are different types of bilingual education programs, some more successful than others. Two-way bilingual programs (also called dual-language programs), have been highly successful. Students in these programs perform as well as, or even better than, students in all-English programs. There are statistics that (4.) <u>back this</u>_____. Most of the two-way bilingual programs are Spanish-English programs, but there are also programs in Korean, French, Navajo, Cantonese, Mandarin Chinese, Arabic, Japanese, Russian, and Portuguese. These are offered mainly in elementary schools. Unfortunately, there are fewer than 200 such programs nationwide.

   While each program is organized differently, they share certain features. Essentially, dual-language programs (5.) <u>boil</u>_____ <u>to</u> this:

   - both languages and both cultures are equally important;
   - native-speakers of each language study together;
   - some academic subjects are taught in English, some in the other language;
   - students act as language and culture experts for each other; and
   - the goal is to speak, understand, read, and write in the two languages.

   Those who are against bilingual education have (6.) <u>lost sight</u>_____ the fact that we are living in a shrinking world. We need to be familiar with more than one language and more than one culture. People in this country need to (7.) <u>set</u>_____ their negative feelings about bilingual education and support an education for the twenty-first century, not one for the twentieth century.

Henry Lopez
Los Angeles, CA, Oct. 10

▶ FOR AN EXTRA CHALLENGE: Discuss your views on bilingual education. Are you <u>for</u> or <u>against</u> it? Why? What do you think of two-way bilingual programs? Use idioms from this chapter in your discussion.

9. **Where Do You Put "It"?**   Read each sentence. If the pronoun object is in the right position, mark *OK*. If the pronoun object is in the wrong position, write in the correct phrase. Compare answers with a partner and try to agree.

1. Education is currently the number one topic in Washington. Democrats and Republicans have been wrangling <u>it</u> over all year.

   OK [ ]   Correction: _____

2. I know you have a lot to say about crime in the cities. Can you sum up <u>it</u> in a few sentences?

   OK [ ]   Correction: _____

3. Sarah has a photograph in that book. Give me the book and I'll point <u>it</u> out to you.

   OK [ ]   Correction: _____

4. If you're having trouble with the first essay question, set aside <u>it</u> until later.

   OK [ ]   Correction: _____

5. On the exam, you need to state the main reasons for homelessness. Try to pin <u>them</u> down first, then discuss what can be done.

   OK [ ]   Correction: _____

6. Don't worry. Whatever you decide to do, we'll back up <u>you</u>.

   OK [ ]   Correction: _____

7. Right now, let's not worry about the little details. Let's not get hung up on <u>them</u>.

   OK [ ]   Correction: _____

⌒ LISTEN IN

10. **Listen and Answer**   Listen to each commercial on the radio. Mark the statement that best describes the commercial.

1. a. [ ] This commercial asks people to draw pictures of the homeless.
    b. [ ] This commercial asks people to think about the homeless and send a check.
    c. [ ] This commercial asks people to work at a homeless shelter.

2. a. [ ] This commercial is for people who don't want to admit that they have an addiction.
    b. [ ] This commercial is for people who are already getting help with their addictions.
    c. [ ] This commercial is for all the people you love.

3. a. [ ] When you need an operation, you have a lot of things to think about. You should discuss all your questions with your doctor at the Surgery Hospital.

   b. [ ] When you need an operation, it's impossible to make a decision about which hospital to go to.

   c. [ ] When you need an operation, the most important decision is to choose the hospital that offers the best surgeons and technology—the Surgery Hospital.

4. a. [ ] The company will teach you how to summarize your work experience.

   b. [ ] The company will help you with medical problems.

   c. [ ] The company will give you work experience before your next job.

5. a. [ ] The company wants to teach you how to do more things in a day.

   b. [ ] The company wants to teach you how to meet new people, so you're not always with your friends and family.

   c. [ ] The company wants to help you make changes so you'll have more time for your friends and family.

Check your answers in the Answer Key on page 192. For ones you found difficult, read the Tapescript on page 178.

11. Listen, Take Notes, and Answer   First look at the questions below. Then listen to the professor's comments about a student's paper and take notes. Finally, answer the questions.

1. What does the professor say the student stated clearly in the essay?

   a. [ ] There are millions of people in the United States.

   b. [ ] Millions of Americans think their lives are going in the wrong direction because they are working to buy things.

   c. [ ] Millions of Americans are working to buy possessions when they want to be traveling.

2. According to the paper, what do these people say consumerism is doing to their lives?

   a. [ ] It's destroying their lives.

   b. [ ] It's making their lives more interesting.

   c. [ ] It's making them volunteer.

3. According to the paper, did Joe Dominguez forget what he wanted in life?

   a. [ ] No, he never knew what he wanted in life.

   b. [ ] Yes, because he loved working on Wall Street and making money.

   c. [ ] No, he never forgot what he wanted in life, and it wasn't making money.

4. What does Joe Dominguez do in his book *Your Money or Your Life*?

   a. [ ] He gives a summary of his ideas on how to make oneself happy.

   b. [ ] He says he doesn't have any idea how to make oneself happy.

   c. [ ] He gives a summary of his ideas on how to start making money right away.

5. What does the professor tell the student to do to make the paper better?

   a. [ ] Describe excessive consumption and explain in general what's wrong with it.

   b. [ ] Summarize voluntary simplicity and state specifically why it's more satisfying than consumption

   c. [ ] State in a general way why voluntary simplicity is better than excessive consumption

6. Why does the professor want the student to find studies about simple lifestyles?

    a. [ ] To show how people can start to live simply

    b. [ ] To show how long people have been living simply

    c. [ ] To show what happens when people live simply over a period of time

7. What does the student ask his readers to do in the paper?

    a. [ ] Change from a consumer lifestyle to simple living

    b. [ ] Spend all their free time shopping to see what the consumer lifestyle is like

    c. [ ] Stop the movement called "voluntary simplicity"

8. What is the professor's opinion about discussing the historical roots of the movement?

    a. [ ] She doesn't want the student to do this.

    b. [ ] She really wants the student to do this.

    c. [ ] She thinks it's OK.

Check your answers in the Answer Key on page 193. For ones you found difficult, read the Tapecript on page 178-179.

SPEAK UP

12. Let's Get Personal   Is this you? For each statement, circle *True* or *False*. Share your answers in a small group. Are the other students in your group just like you?

1. When I'm in a group, I don't like to draw attention to myself.   True   False

2. I'm not the type of person who likes to wrangle over politics.   True   False

3. I would never set aside my political views for someone I loved.   True   False

4. If I think a close friend is on the wrong track in life, I always tell him or her.
True   False

5. My parents have always backed me up, no matter what I've wanted to do.
True   False

6. It's hard for me to come to terms with my bad habits.   True   False

7. For me, learning English boils down to lots of hard work.   True   False

8. When I make a mistake in English, I like it when someone points it out to me.
True   False

9. I never get hung up on what I'm going to wear.   True   False

10. I have nothing against American food.   True   False

FOR AN EXTRA CHALLENGE: After sharing your answers, go back and circle the idiom in each sentence. Check your answers in the Answer Key on page 193.

13. **Act It Out: A Support Group**   In groups of 3, act out the conversations. One person presents a problem to the group. The others make suggestions for solving the problem using as many idioms as they can from the list on pages 94-95. Make any changes you find necessary, for example, change *wife* to *husband*.

Problem 1: My parents are constantly pointing out all the things I do wrong. I've asked them to stop, but they won't. It's very annoying.

Problem 2: My wife and I used to have so much fun together when we first got married. We used to make plans to do all sorts of things, such as travel to different countries, buy a boat, and take dancing lessons. But now it's all work and no play. We seem to have lost sight of those wonderful plans.

Problem 3: Recently, my best friend drew my attention to the fact that I spend all my free time shopping. She also made the point that, with all that shopping, I'm probably spending all my money and not saving anything. I have to admit that she's right, but I'm not sure I can change. I think I'm what's called a compulsive shopper.

 ## WRITE IT OUT

14. **Create a Letter to the Editor**   Read the newspaper headlines. Choose the one that interests you. Find a partner who chose the same headline. Together, write a letter to the editor about the topic of the headline using as many idioms as you can from the list on pages 94-95. Then read your letter to the class.

Teachers Draw Attention to Rising Test Scores

Senators Wrangle over Government Help for the Poor

The Internet Is Wreaking Havoc with Family Life

Coming to Terms with Violence on TV

Religious Group Pins Down Problems with Divorce

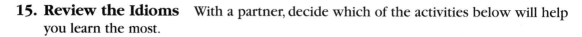

15. Review the Idioms   With a partner, decide which of the activities below will help you learn the most.

- Write the meaning of each idiom.

- Write a sample sentence for each idiom.

- Give examples of subjects and/or objects that go with each idiom. (Note: Not all idioms require objects.)

  EXAMPLE: <u>This class</u> has almost wrapped up <u>this chapter</u>.
                  s   o

- Practice saying the idioms with correct stress. (Verbs and adverbs/particles are stressed, but the verbs *to be* and *to have* and one-syllable prepositions are not stressed.) If possible, practice saying the idioms in sentences.

Then use the list that follows to help you complete the activities together. Note the two symbols for objects.

> ( ) = The object of the preposition. It goes after the preposition.
> [ ] = The object of the phrasal verb. If it is a pronoun, it goes between the verb and adverb/particle. If it is a noun, it can go between the verb and the adverb/particle *or* after the adverb/particle.

1. back [ ] up _____

_____

2. be on the wrong track _____

_____

3. boil down to ( ) _____

_____

4. come to terms with ( ) _____

_____

5. draw attention to ( ); draw one's attention to ( ) _____

_____

6. get hung up on ( ) _____

_____

Usage: Very informal

7. have nothing against ( ); have something against ( ) _____

_____

_____
Usage: Informal
8. lose sight of ( ) _____

_____

9. make a point; make the point that _____

_____

10. pin [ ] down _____

_____

11. play out _____

_____

12. point [ ] out; point [ ] out to ( ) _____

_____

13. set [ ] aside _____

_____

14. sum [ ] up _____

_____

15. wrangle over ( ) _____

_____

16. wreak havoc with ( ) _____

_____

7 ANGER

GETTING STARTED

1. Share Your Reactions   In a small group, discuss the following statistics and questions about homelessness. Share your answers with the class.

THE HOMELESS IN THE UNITED STATES

- On any night, about 700,000 people are living on the street in the United States.
- In one year, up to two million people are homeless.
- The average homeless person lives on the street seven years.
- One-third of all homeless people are families.
- The fastest-growing group of homeless is children.
- In 1981 there were thirty soup kitchens in New York City. In 1990 there were 700.

Sources: National Coalition for the Homeless; National Law Center on Homelessness and Poverty; *Harper's Index*.

1. How should governments solve the problem of homelessness?

2. What would you do if a homeless person asked you for money?

3. What is the best way to learn more about the homeless?

INTRODUCTION OF IDIOMS

2. Read Between the Lines Read the journal entries. With a partner, try to understand what they mean. Then do Exercise 3.

Coping with Homelessness

January 19th, Day 1

Yesterday, I went to Houston Street in lower Manhattan and bought some used clothes for nineteen dollars. Today, I changed into them in the men's room at Penn Station. When I placed my own clothes in a locker, I closed the door on the world I knew. For ten days, I would try to **cope with** another world. I would learn firsthand what it was like to be homeless in America.

In my new, old clothes, I became invisible to most people walking past me. Only a few men my own age **made eye contact** and perhaps wondered what had happened to me.

In a coffee shop, I discovered that waiters in New York didn't trust the homeless. They made us pay first, but let the other patrons pay when finished. After it happened to me a few times, I **was** pretty **fed up with** this treatment. However, I had no choice but to **put up with** it.

Hoping to spend my first night in Penn Station, I discovered the police had other ideas. I was politely escorted out of the building. I walked up to **47th** Street, where I knew there was a warm grate on which to sleep.

January 21, Day 3

Two men threatened to **beat me up** if I didn't **hand over** my money. Without thinking, I ran. Fortunately, they didn't follow me.

January 24, Day 6

Cold temperatures drove me into the Men's Shelter at East 3rd Street today. The shelter serves meals to 1,300 people every day. The smells and noise were oppressive, the atmosphere tense. Men fought about their "space," and their place in line. Three or four police officers were constantly **breaking up** fights and telling the men to **calm down**. And, as if things weren't bad enough, some of the supervisors seemed to enjoy **dishing out** insults along with the food.

As I looked around the room, I found that drugs and alcohol were common among these men. I figured that about half of them could never work. Addiction, homelessness, poverty, and illness had **taken their toll.**

January 25, Day 7

Today, in the East Village, a band of musicians was performing on the street. It was one of the few diversions that could **take** my **mind off** my situation. Although I wanted to dance to the music, I couldn't let myself.

With little to do now, I find myself watching the real homeless. While many are filled with anger, others accept their fate without complaint. Once, when I was in a coffee shop and a waiter told me to **get out**, I successfully appealed to the owner, who had seen me before. But I realize that because many street people lack self-respect and **feel out of place**, most simply would have gathered their bags and left.

January 27, Day 9

At the shelters, everybody **gets on** each other's **nerves**. Anything you do is interpreted as **asking for trouble**. For example, yesterday I rested my foot on the rung of the chair in front of me. The young man sitting there told me to **cut it out**. Then he informed a much bigger and angrier friend, who **blew up** and threatened to punish me later. Fearing a surprise attack during the night, I wrote my name, address, and telephone number on a piece of paper and slipped it into my pocket in case I was beaten senseless.

January 28, Day 10

I left the shelter early to avoid another conflict. Clearly, at the shelters, the issues of anger and respect simmer just below the surface.

On my last night, after being **kicked out** of both the bus terminal and Grand Central Station, I returned to my locker at Penn Station, changed back into my own clothes, and took the subway uptown to my home.

Note: John Coleman was a college president for ten years before his experiment with homelessness. These journal entries were based on an article he wrote about the experiment, "Diary of a Homeless Man."

UNDERSTANDING THE MEANING

3. **Line by Line**   With a partner, mark the answer that explains the journal entries on pages 97–98. Then look at the journal entries and find the sentence or phrase with the same meaning. Write that sentence or phrase below. (Note: One question requires two sentences.)

1. How was John Coleman going to learn about homelessness?

   a. [ ] He was going to find a homeless man, interview him, and then write an article.
   b. [ ] He was going to personally struggle with homelessness for ten days.
   c. [ ] He was going to help the homeless in America.

   Sentence: _____

2. How did people behave toward Coleman?

   a. [ ] Some men looked in his eyes and wondered why he was homeless.
   b. [ ] Most people looked at him and wondered why he was homeless.
   c. [ ] Some people tried to talk with him because they wondered why he was homeless.

   Sentence: _____

3. How did Coleman feel about the way the waiters in New York treated the homeless?

   a. [ ] It didn't bother him at all.
   b. [ ] It bothered him a little bit.
   c. [ ] It bothered him a lot.

   Sentence: _____

4. What did Coleman do about the waiters' treatment?

   a. [ ] He complained, then ate his food and left.
   b. [ ] He had to accept it, even though he didn't like it.
   c. [ ] He fought with the waiters.

   Sentence: _____

5. What did the police do constantly at the Men's Shelter?

   a. [ ] They put some of the homeless men in jail for fighting and arguing.
   b. [ ] They stopped the fights and told the homeless men to relax.
   c. [ ] They helped the staff cook and serve food to the homeless.

   Sentence: _____

6. How did the concert on the street affect John Coleman?

   a. [ ] It helped him forget his experiment for a while.
   b. [ ] It changed his attitude about the homeless.
   c. [ ] It helped him become interested in music.

   Sentence: _____

7. What happened to Coleman in a coffee shop one day?

    a. [ ] A waiter told him to sit in the back.

    b. [ ] A waiter told him to ask the owner if he could eat there.

    c. [ ] A waiter told him to leave.

    Sentence: _____

8. What did the man say when Coleman put his foot on the rung of the man's chair?

    a. [ ] He told Coleman to stop it.

    b. [ ] He told Coleman he would cut him with a knife.

    c. [ ] He told Coleman to go outside.

    Sentence: _____

9. What happened on Coleman's last night?

    a. [ ] He was forced to leave two public places.

    b. [ ] He kicked someone at the bus terminal.

    c. [ ] He was forced to sleep at Penn Station.

    Sentence: _____

4. **Paraphrase the E-mail Message**   Read the e-mail message describing Coleman's experiment below. Work with a partner. For each idiom in bold, find the meaning in the box at the top of page 101. Write the letter of the idiom next to its meaning.

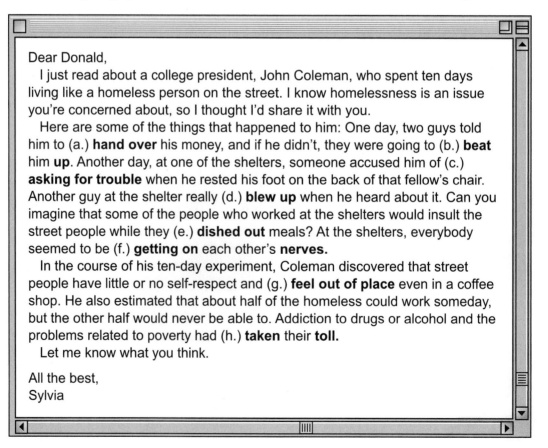

Dear Donald,

   I just read about a college president, John Coleman, who spent ten days living like a homeless person on the street. I know homelessness is an issue you're concerned about, so I thought I'd share it with you.

   Here are some of the things that happened to him: One day, two guys told him to (a.) **hand over** his money, and if he didn't, they were going to (b.) **beat him up**. Another day, at one of the shelters, someone accused him of (c.) **asking for trouble** when he rested his foot on the back of that fellow's chair. Another guy at the shelter really (d.) **blew up** when he heard about it. Can you imagine that some of the people who worked at the shelters would insult the street people while they (e.) **dished out** meals? At the shelters, everybody seemed to be (f.) **getting on** each other's **nerves**.

   In the course of his ten-day experiment, Coleman discovered that street people have little or no self-respect and (g.) **feel out of place** even in a coffee shop. He also estimated that about half of the homeless could work someday, but the other half would never be able to. Addiction to drugs or alcohol and the problems related to poverty had (h.) **taken** their **toll**.

   Let me know what you think.

All the best,
Sylvia

_____ 1. looking for a fight

_____ 2. annoying

_____ 3. give

_____ 4. are uncomfortable in a situation

_____ 5. done a lot of damage

_____ 6. exploded with anger

_____ 7. distributed

_____ 8. hit and hurt

NEW CONTEXTS

5. Fill In the Missing Idioms   Read the editorial from a suburban newspaper. With a partner, fill in each blank with an idiom from the box. (Note: *cope with* and *put up with* have the same meaning and are interchangeable.) Then discuss your reaction to road rage.

Road Rage

Every morning, along country roads, animals run for cover. The sounds of nature have been replaced by the sounds of automobiles: Engines race, tires screech, horns blare. In their Explorers and Voyagers, drivers are cursing, screaming, honking, and (1.) _____ insults at their fellow drivers, all in an effort to make them drive faster, turn quicker, and move as soon as the light turns green.

Road rage is spreading along these back roads like a virus. In the race to get to work, get to school, or get to the gym, drivers are (2.) _____. Consideration for others is being tossed out the window. They can't (3.) _____ cautious kids. They won't (4.) _____ slow-paced pedestrians. They (5.) _____ feeble folks.

The pressure of modern life is (6.) _____. With more and more people driving faster and faster, we're all (7.) _____. Unless we can (8.) _____ and stop expressing our anger through aggressive driving, there will be more unnecessary accidents. Road rage—do something about it before it's too late.

are fed up with	*dishing out*
asking for trouble	*getting on each other's nerves*
calm down	*put up with*
cope with	*taking its toll*

6. Figure It Out   Mark the answer that is closest in meaning to each idiom. Compare answers with a partner and try to agree.

SITUATION I: One friend telling another about a robbery at work

1. Joan: I was at work today when a man came into the bank and said to me, "**Hand over** all the money in the drawer, or else."
   a. [ ] Count   b. [ ] Give me   c. [ ] Show me

2. Paulette: How frightening! How long did it take you to **calm down** afterwards?
   a. [ ] call the police   b. [ ] make yourself peaceful   c. [ ] lie on the floor

SITUATION II: A husband and wife discussing their relationship

3. Husband: I just don't understand why you have to **blow up over** every little thing.
   a. [ ] breathe hard for   b. [ ] discuss   c. [ ] get angry about

4. Wife: Every little thing? Look, it's your flirtatious behavior that I'**m fed up with**.
   a. [ ] am very tired of   b. [ ] am very jealous of   c. [ ] am very pleased with

SITUATION III: A couple reading the local newspaper at breakfast

5. Woman: Look at this! Three boys were **kicked out of** school last week.
   a. [ ] in a fight at   b. [ ] forced to leave   c. [ ] absent from

6. Man: Yes, I heard. Apparently, they **beat up** another boy on the playground.
   a. [ ] hit and hurt badly   b. [ ] teased and hurt   c. [ ] ran after

SITUATION IV: Two students discussing a student demonstration

7. Melissa: It was really scary when the police came to **break up** the demonstration.
   a. [ ] arrest people at   b. [ ] speak at   c. [ ] stop

8. Elaine: Yeah, I can't **take** my **mind off** it. I didn't know what was going to happen.
   a. [ ] look the other way   b. [ ] think about other things   c. [ ] understand

SITUATION V: Two employees discussing their new boss

9. Michael: Have you noticed that the new vice president never **makes eye contact** when he's talking to you?
   a. [ ] closes his eyes   b. [ ] wears contact lenses   c. [ ] looks at your eyes

10. Ryan: Strange, isn't it? I think he really **feels out of place** here.
    a. [ ] is uncomfortable   b. [ ] wants to work   c. [ ] doesn't like it

7. **Information Gap: Role Play**   Work with a partner. Student A follows the directions below. At the same time, Student B turns to pages 171–172 and follows the directions there.

At the same time, Student B turns to pages 171–172 and follows the directions there.

Student A's Directions, Part 1

Read the description of the scene below. Then read Anita's lines silently. (Do not show these lines to your partner.) Decide which one comes first and read it out loud to your partner. Your partner will then look for a line in his or her script that goes next. Then find your next line. Continue back and forth until you've used all your lines. Finally, put the lines in order by writing the number of the line (1–4) next to each one.

Description of the Scene

In a television studio, a soap opera is being taped. Two actors playing the roles of Anita and Luke are doing a scene. Luke is holding an envelope and staring at the ceiling. Anita is standing in front of him, looking angry. She wants Luke to give her the envelope. Anita speaks first.

Anita's Lines

____ a. **Calm down**?! I can't **cope with** this. Your behavior is **getting on** my **nerves**. And I want that letter, now.

____ b. (*Holding her hand out for the letter*) OK, Luke, **hand** it **over**.

____ c. I should **kick** you **out**. I don't know why I **put up with** you.

____ d. How are we supposed to discuss our problems when you won't even **make eye contact with** me?

Student A's Directions, Part 2

Read the description of the scene below. Then read Shelley's lines silently. (Do not show these lines to your partner.) After you hear the father's first line, decide which one of Shelley's lines comes first and read it out loud to your partner. Your partner will then look for the line in his or her script that goes next. Then find your next line. Continue back and forth until you've used all your lines. Then put the lines in order by writing the number of the line (1–4) next to each one. Finally, choose one of the scenes (Part 1 or Part 2) and perform it in front of the class.

Description of the Scene

Shelley, age 17, has just come home from a night out. She is putting her coat away in the front hall when her father comes down the stairs, dressed in his bathrobe and slippers. Her father speaks first.

Shelley's Lines

____ f. What? The car keys? **Cut it out**, Dad. You're **getting on** my **nerves**.

____ g. OK, Dad, here are the keys. At least you didn't threaten to **kick** me **out** this time.

____ h. No, I don't know what time it is, but I hope you're not going to **blow up** again.

____ i. Oh, Dad, **calm down**. I'm only 45 minutes late.

GETTING IT RIGHT

8. **Where Do You Put "It"?**   Read each sentence. If the pronoun object is in the right position, mark *OK*. If the pronoun object is in the wrong position, write in the correct phrase. Compare answers with a partner.

1. Please stop teasing your brother. Cut <u>it</u> out!

   OK [ ]   Correction: _____

2. When the police officer stopped the driver for speeding, she asked him for his license and registration. But the driver didn't want to hand over <u>them</u>.

   OK [ ]   Correction: _____

3. Two young boys had a fistfight in the school cafeteria yesterday. One of the teachers had to break <u>it</u> up.

   OK [ ]   Correction: _____

4. How can you continue to work twelve-hour days? I don't know how you cope with <u>it</u>.

   OK [ ]   Correction: _____

5. The older boy was just joking with the younger one. He wasn't going to beat up <u>him</u>.

   OK [ ]   Correction: _____

6. She was so nervous before the exam she had to take a walk to calm <u>herself</u> down.

   OK [ ]   Correction: _____

LISTEN IN

9. **Listen, Take Notes, and Answer**   First look at the questions below. Then listen to the lecture in a college course in psychology. The professor is presenting research studies on stress. Take notes while you listen. Finally, answer the questions.

1. In the beginning of the presentation, what does the professor want the students to think about?

   a. [ ] How to stop stress in their lives
   b. [ ] How well they manage stress in their lives
   c. [ ] Why they have so much stress in their lives

2. The professor asks the class to think about their reactions to certain everyday situations. What does she want to know?

   a. [ ] Whether they are nervous in class or not
   b. [ ] Whether the situations upset them or not
   c. [ ] Whether they like to drive or not

3. According to the professor, what did the recent study discover about the effects of angry responses on the young?

    a. [ ] They have no effect on their health later.
    b. [ ] They have a good effect on their health later.
    c. [ ] They have a bad effect on their health later.

4. Based on what the professor said, what do you think people should do when they start to get angry?

    a. [ ] They should beat someone up.
    b. [ ] They should dish out insults.
    c. [ ] They should try to calm themselves.

5. What is the professor going to talk about next?

    a. [ ] A study showing that women who get upset easily will have health problems later
    b. [ ] A study examining what is annoying to women
    c. [ ] A study showing why women should express their anger more

Check your answers in the Answer Key on page 193. For ones you found difficult, read the Tapescript on page 179.

10. Listen and Summarize A woman and her husband are having an argument. Listen to the woman. Then write a summary of what she says. Use idioms from this chapter in your summary. Read your summary to a partner and try to agree.

 ## SPEAK UP

11. Let's Get Personal Is this you? For each statement, circle *True* or *False*. Share your answers in a small group. Are the other students in your group just like you?

1. When I want to take my mind off something, I watch television.   True   False

2. I usually make eye contact with people when I speak to them.   True   False

3. When I was young, I always used to get on my parents' nerves.   True   False

4. I often blow up over small problems.   True   False

5. When I need to calm down, I do deep breathing or meditate.   True   False

6. I usually cope with stress very well.   True   False

7. If I don't like what a friend is doing, I tell that person to cut it out.   True   False

8. When I'm with people from another country, I sometimes feel out of place. True   False

9. I can't put up with rude people.   True   False

10. I've never been kicked out of school.   True   False

► FOR AN EXTRA CHALLENGE: After sharing your answers, go back and circle the idiom in each sentence. Check your answers in the Answer Key on page 193.

12. **Act It Out: A Support Group**   In groups of three, act out the conversations. One person presents a problem to the group. The others make suggestions for solving the problem using as many idioms as they can from the list on pages 107–108. Make any changes you find necessary, for example, change *wife* to *husband*.

Problem 1: I was kicked out of my apartment because my rent was raised and I couldn't afford the higher rent. Now I'm back living with my parents and four brothers and sisters. After living alone, I really feel out of place there. I have no privacy. And it's taking its toll on my schoolwork.

Problem 2: My supervisor always wants to know what's happening in my personal life and dishes out advice all the time. I'm really fed up with the whole situation. I don't know how much longer I can put up with it. It's really taking its toll on my work.

Problem 3: Someone who works at the desk next to mine makes personal phone calls all the time and talks very loudly. It really gets on my nerves. I don't know what to do. I can't cope with this situation any longer.

WRITE IT OUT

13. **Create a News Story**   Read the newspaper headlines. Choose the one that interests you. Find a partner who chose the same headline. Together, write a news story that goes with the headline, using as many idioms as you can from the list on pages 107–108. Then read your story to the class.

> *Three Teenagers Asking for Trouble in Local Shopping Mall*

> *President Blows Up over Rumors of an Affair*

> *Police Break Up Student Demonstration*

> *American Journalists Told to Get Out of War Zone*

> *Minority Students Still Feel Out of Place on Some College Campuses*

14. Review the Idioms   With a partner, decide which of the activities below will help you learn the most.

- Write the meaning of each idiom.

- Write a sample sentence for each idiom.

- Give examples of subjects and/or objects that go with each idiom.
  (Note: Not all idioms require objects.)

  EXAMPLE: <u>This class</u> has almost wrapped up <u>this chapter</u>.
                         s   o

- Practice saying the idioms with correct stress. (Verbs and adverbs/particles are stressed, but the verbs *to be* and *to have* and one-syllable prepositions are not stressed.) If possible, practice saying the idioms in sentences.

Then use the list that follows to help you complete the activities together. Note the two symbols for objects.

> ( ) = The object of the preposition. It goes after the preposition.
>
> [ ] = The object of the phrasal verb. If it is a pronoun, it goes between the verb and adverb/particle. If it is a noun, it can go between the verb and the adverb/particle *or* after the adverb/particle.

1. ask for trouble _____

_____

2. beat [ ] up _____

_____

3. be fed up; be fed up with ( ) _____

_____

Usage: Also become/get fed up; become/get fed up with

4. blow up; blow up over ( ) _____

_____

5. break [ ] up _____

_____

6. calm down; calm [ ] down _____

_____

Usage: Informal

7. cope with ( ) _____

_____
Usage: Often negative: He can't cope with his job.

8. cut it out _____

_____
Usage: Informal.

9. dish [ ] out _____

_____
Usage: Informal

10. feel out of place _____

_____

11. get on one's nerves _____

_____
Usage: Informal; also get on each other's nerves

12. get out; get out of ( ) _____

_____
Usage: Informal

13. hand [ ] over _____

_____
Usage: Informal; often imperative: Hand it over!

14. kick [ ] out; kick [ ] out of ( ) _____

_____
Usage: Informal; often passive voice: He was kicked out of college.

15. make eye contact; make eye contact with ( ) _____

_____

_____
Usage: Also have eye contact with

16. put up with ( ) _____

_____

17. take its toll; take its toll on ( ) _____

_____

18. take one's mind off ( ) _____

_____

Chapter 8

DRIVING AND DIRECTIONS

GETTING STARTED

1. **Answer the Survey**   Write your answers to the following survey questions. Then interview a partner and write his/her answers. Discuss your answers.

My answers	My partner's answers
1. How important is a car to you? [ ] Very important. [ ] A little important. [ ] Not very important. [ ] Not important at all.	1. How important is a car to you? [ ] Very important. [ ] A little important. [ ] Not very important. [ ] Not important at all.
2. If you drive a car, how do you usually drive? [ ] Over the speed limit (fast) [ ] At the speed limit (average) [ ] Under the speed limit (slowly)	2. If you drive a car, how do you usually drive? [ ] Over the speed limit (fast) [ ] At the speed limit (average) [ ] Under the speed limit (slowly)
3. Can you follow directions easily? [ ] Yes [ ] No	3. Can you follow directions easily? [ ] Yes [ ] No
4. Who do you think drives better? [ ] Women [ ] Men	4. Who do you think drives better? [ ] Women [ ] Men
5. What do you think of the drivers in your city or town? [ ] They're dangerous drivers. [ ] They're cautious drivers. [ ] They're good drivers.	5. What do you think of the drivers in your city or town? [ ] They're dangerous drivers. [ ] They're cautious drivers. [ ] They're good drivers.

INTRODUCTION OF IDIOMS

2. **Read Between the Lines**   Read the directions for the road rallye, a long-distance automobile race on public roads. With a partner, try to understand what it says and mark the route on the map on page 111. If you don't understand an idiom, look at pages 112–113. Work quickly.

Write your starting time now: _____.

Keep on Going

Directions for the Road Rallye

1. **Start out** in the parking lot of the Hopewell Hotel. Leave the lot and **make a right** onto Allegheny Avenue. Make another right immediately and drive to Crosby Street. Turn right at Monument Circle. Go three-quarters of the way around the circle and turn right. Turn left onto Delano Boulevard East. **Slow down** and **pull into** the first gas station you see.

    Checkpoint 1: What kind of gas is it? _____
    (If you're not sure, see the answer in the Answer Key on page 194.)

2. After you **fill up** the tank, **pull out of** the gas station onto Delano. Go west on Second Street until you see Bethlehem Street. Turn left and **head for** Tunnel Road. Drive down Tunnel Road. **Make a left** onto Hemlock Drive.

    Checkpoint 2: Where are you? _____
    (If you're not sure, see the answer in the Answer Key on page 194.)

3. **Turn around** and take Hemlock Drive back toward Tunnel Road. Turn right, then turn right onto River Road heading east. Turn left and cross the bridge over the river. **Take a left** onto Wharf Street. Then turn right onto Bethlehem. In the middle of the next block, **pull over** across from the government building with a flag in front.

    Checkpoint 3: What building is it? _____
    (If you're not sure, see the answer in the Answer Key on page 194.)

4. **Keep on going** to the end of Bethlehem. Go right and continue until you see a fast-food restaurant. Stop in the parking lot.

    Checkpoint 4: What is the name of the restaurant? _____
    (If you're not sure, see the answer in the Answer Key on page 194.)

5. Come out of the lot and turn right onto Crosby Street. If the street is **blocked off**, **back up** into the parking lot and take Crosby in the opposite direction. Turn right on Third Street. **Watch out**—if there's a deer in the middle of the road, don't **run it over**. Turn around and go west on Third. Make a left onto Allegheny and pass Second Street. Make a left after the parking lot and **pull up** in front of the drug store.

    Checkpoint 5: Where did you **end up**? _____
    (If you're not sure, see the answer in the Answer Key on page 194.)

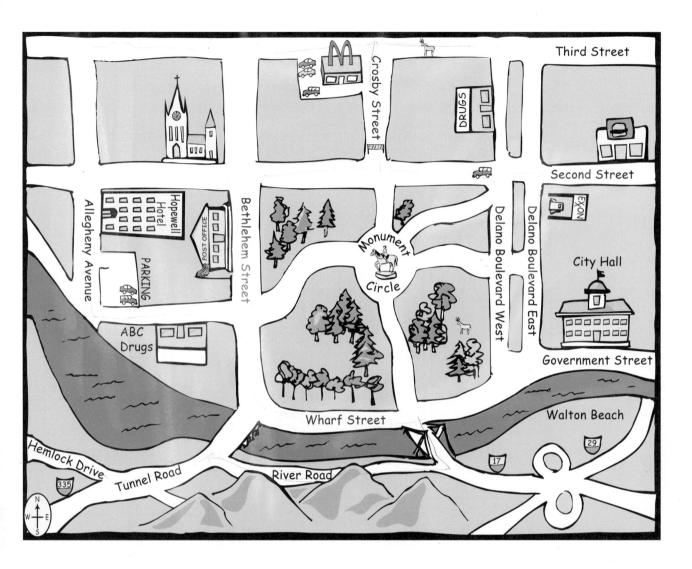

Congratulations! You've reached the end of the road rallye. Write your end time below. How long did the rallye take? Compare your time with that of other teams. Did you **make good time** compared to other teams? Did you have a good time?

End time: _____   Total time: _____

3. Picture It The drawings below will help you understand the meaning of each idiom in the directions for the road rallye.

head for   *block off*   *back up*   *end up*

pull into   *pull up*   *fill up*

keep on going   *turn around*

pull out of

take a left

run over

slow down

pull over

start out

make a right

watch out

make good time

4. **Match It Up**   Read each line of conversation between two friends, Jeff and Takashi. Jeff is telling Takashi about the road rallye. Takashi doesn't say much; he mostly paraphrases what Jeff says. With a partner, write the letter of each of Takashi's responses next to Jeff's lines.

JEFF

____ 1. In a road rallye, you have to **start out** in a particular place and **end up** in a certain place at each checkpoint.

____ 2. Yes. One of the first things we had to do was **make a right** onto Allegheny Avenue.

____ 3. Uh-huh. At the first checkpoint, we had to **slow down** and **pull into** a gas station.

____ 4. Right. After **filling up** the tank, we had to **pull out of** the gas station and go west on Second Street.

____ 5. Yes, then at Bethlehem Street, we **headed for** the tunnel.

____ 6. Right. The tunnel led to the park, but then **we turned around**, went over the bridge, and **took a left**.

____ 7. Eventually, we **pulled over** across the street from a big government building.

TAKASHI

a. You mean during the race, you had to go slower and drive into a gas station?

b. Then you drove in the direction of the tunnel?

c. Later, you drove to the side of the road and stopped.

d. So you drove to the park, but then you had to drive in the opposite direction, cross the bridge, and turn left. I see.

e. You mean you have to begin where you are told and finally arrive at a particular place at each checkpoint?

f. I see. After getting gas, you drove out of the gas station and went west.

g. At the beginning of the rallye, you had to turn right?

5. Sign Language Under each road sign, write the sentence with the same meaning from the box. Compare answers with a partner and try to agree.

1. _____

2. _____

3. _____

4. _____

a. Take the next exit if you want to **turn around**.

b. People are doing roadwork. **Slow down**!

c. Be careful not to **run over** a deer.

d. You're not allowed to **make a left**.

6. **Figure It Out**   Mark the answer that is closest in meaning to each idiom. Compare answers with a partner and try to agree.

SITUATION I: A woman and man are at a train station. The woman is leaning over the platform trying to see the train.

1. Woman: I can't believe I missed the train! It must have **pulled out of** the station early.

   a. [ ] moved closer to   b. [ ] arrived at   c. [ ] left

2. Man: **Watch out**! Here comes another train.

   a. [ ] Be careful!   b. [ ] Look at the schedule!   c. [ ] Look at the time!

SITUATION II: Two people talking about a marathon, a 26.2-mile foot race

3. Woman: Runners in the New York City Marathon **start out in** Staten Island and run through Manhattan, Brooklyn, the Bronx, and Queens.

   a. [ ] finish   b. [ ] begin   c. [ ] continue

4. Man: They **end up in** Manhattan, don't they?

   a. [ ] finish   b. [ ] begin   c. [ ] continue

SITUATION III: Two people in a car

5. Passenger: I thought you were **headed for** the highway.

   a. [ ] going away from   b. [ ] thinking about taking
   c. [ ] going in the direction of

6. Driver: I'd better **pull into** this gas station before we get on the highway. We need gas.

   a. [ ] ask for directions at   b. [ ] drive toward and enter
   c. [ ] get gas and pay at

SITUATION IV: Two people in a car

7. Driver: I think we're lost. Maybe I should **turn around** as soon as I can.

   a. [ ] look for a map   b. [ ] drive in the opposite direction
   c. [ ] stop the car on the side of the road

8. Passenger: **Pull up** so I can see the street sign. Then I'll see where we are on the map.

   a. [ ] Drive forward a little   b. [ ] Drive to the side of the road   c. [ ] Stop here

SITUATION V: A new driver and an inspector during a road test

9. Driver: Did you say you want me to **make a left** at this corner?

   a. [ ] park on the left   b. [ ] turn to the left   c. [ ] leave the car

10. Inspector: Yes, then I want you to park behind that minivan. I want to see you **back up**.

    a. [ ] turn the wheel   b. [ ] go forward   c. [ ] go in reverse

7. What Would You Do? Read each situation below and mark your answer. In a small group, share your answers. Report the results to the class.

1. You're driving to an important job interview and you don't have a lot of time. Suddenly you realize you need gas. You stop at a gas station to **fill up** the tank, but there's a long line. What do you do?

   a. [ ] Wait in line even if it means you'll be late for your interview.
   b. [ ] Cut in front of somebody in line.
   c. [ ] Continue driving and hope that you have enough gas to get there.
   d. [ ] Other: _____

2. This morning, you have an appointment to take an exam for a new job. On the way to the company, you notice that a road you need to take has been **blocked off** by the police. You don't know your way around the neighborhood. What do you do?

   a. [ ] Try to find another way to get to the company.
   b. [ ] Call the personnel office that is running the test and say you'll be late because the road is closed.
   c. [ ] Move the police barricade away and drive down the road to take the test.
   d. [ ] Other: _____

3. Today is your first day at a new job. On the way to work, you see an elderly driver **pull over** and fall forward on the steering wheel. There's nobody around. What do you do?

   a. [ ] Stop and help the driver, even if it means you will be late on your first day.
   b. [ ] Continue driving until you see a public telephone. Call emergency medical services for the driver. Then go to work.
   c. [ ] Continue driving to work and hope that somebody else stops to help the driver.
   d. [ ] Other: _____

8. It's News to Me Read each example of authentic language taken from newspapers and magazines and try to notice the idiom. With a partner, discuss the meaning of each idiom in that particular context. Some meanings may be figurative, not literal. Write the idiom and its meaning below.

1. From an article in *People* magazine about Bill Cosby, the comedian, actor, and writer:

   > At 61, Cosby, who lives in Manhattan with Camille, his wife of 35 years, is busier than ever. He stars in two CBS shows, writes a children's book series, recently bought an interest in the NBA's New Jersey Nets—and shows no sign of slowing down.

   _____ = _____

2. From an article in *The New York Times* about taxicab drivers using cell phones:

> Taxi and Limousine Commission . . . officials said yesterday that they were drafting a rule that would outlaw cellular conversations by drivers unless their cars are pulled over and stopped.

_____ = _____

3. From an article in *The New York Times* on the need for Americans to study science:

> Any American undergraduate today who considers physics as a career soon realizes that [upon] finishing five or six tough years of graduate work, he or she would be faced with a tight job market in which low salaries are the norm.
>
> Many physics Ph.D.'s end up on Wall Street, where they do computer work and data analysis for much better pay than they would get as physicists.

_____ = _____

▶ GETTING IT RIGHT

9. **Where Do You Put "It"?**   Read each sentence. If the pronoun object is in the right position, mark *OK*. If the pronoun object is in the wrong position, write in the correct phrase. Compare answers with a partner and try to agree.

1. Wow! He left that parking space in a hurry. Did you see how fast he pulled out of <u>it</u>?

   OK [ ]   Correction: _____

2. When he buys gas, he always says, "Fill <u>it</u> up."

   OK [ ]   Correction: _____

3. Your car is too far from the gas pump. Would you pull up <u>it</u> a little?

   OK [ ]   Correction: _____

4. If you don't turn the car around, I'm going home. Turn around <u>it</u>, or I'll get out and walk.

   OK [ ]   Correction: _____

5. We warned him about that huge pothole in Newport Beach, but he ended <u>it</u> up in anyway.

   OK [ ]   Correction: _____

LISTEN IN

10. Listen and Paraphrase   Listen to each recorded message. Mark the statement that correctly paraphrases what was said.

1. a. [ ] You should park on the street, not in the driveway.
   b. [ ] You should come in and park in the driveway.
   c. [ ] You should drive away after the party.

2. a. [ ] The man wants his wife to pack the car for their trip.
   b. [ ] The man wants his wife to leave the car in the parking lot.
   c. [ ] The man wants his wife to get the car and get gas before their trip.

3. a. [ ] You can stop in the middle of the road for a short time to let passengers out.
   b. [ ] You should let passengers out near the sidewalk and stay with your car.
   c. [ ] After letting passengers out of your car, you should pull their suitcases to the sidewalk quickly.

4. a. [ ] Be careful as you leave the parking lot of the Suburban Mall.
   b. [ ] Use caution when entering the Suburban Mall's parking lot.
   c. [ ] The Suburban Mall is very busy. Be careful while parking.

5. a. [ ] When you come for a road test, start a new line and wait for the test to begin.
   b. [ ] Road tests begin on Twelfth Street.
   c. [ ] To take a road test, drive to Elm Street where the test begins.

Check your answers in the Answer Key on page 194. For ones you found difficult, read the Tapescript on page 180.

11. Listen and Answer   The following conversations are taking place in cars. Listen to each conversation and the question that follows it. Read the three choices and mark the one that answers the question correctly.

1. a. [ ] He'll go in reverse right away.
   b. [ ] He'll continue driving, and then make a U-turn.
   c. [ ] He'll block the car that's behind him.

2. a. [ ] He's worried that the dog will attack the driver.
   b. [ ] He's worried that the driver will hit the dog.
   c. [ ] He's worried about the time.

3. a. [ ] They should arrive late.
   b. [ ] They should go to the party right away to avoid the traffic later.
   c. [ ] They should stay until the end of the party.

4. a. [ ] The scenic route
   b. [ ] Route 206
   c. [ ] Going to the right

5. a. [ ] She asks if she should go forward a little after parking.
   b. [ ] She asks if she needs a bigger parking space.
   c. [ ] She asks if she should drive more slowly.

Check your answers in the Answer Key on page 194. For ones you found difficult, read the Tapescript on page 180.

SPEAK UP

12. **Let's Get Personal**   Is this you? For each statement, circle *True* or *False*. Share your answers in a small group. Are the other students in your group just like you?

   1. I like it when streets are blocked off to traffic so pedestrians can walk in the middle of the street.   True   False

   2. I think drivers should pull over when they're talking on cell phones.   True   False

   3. Sometimes I forget to look behind me before backing up.   True   False

   4. Once when I was going to a party, I ended up at the wrong house.   True   False

   5. My friends sometimes forget to fill up the tank when they need gas.   True   False

   6. When I was learning how to drive, I didn't like to turn around.   True   False

   7. When I'm in a car, I don't care if I make good time or not.   True   False

   8. I think it's good to slow down when you see a police car, even if you're not speeding.   True   False

   9. When I'm taking a trip by car, I prefer to start out early in the morning. True   False

   10. If there's something wrong with your car, I think it's a good idea to keep on going until you find a gas station.   True   False

   FOR AN EXTRA CHALLENGE: After sharing your answers, go back and circle the idiom in each sentence. Check your answers in the Answer Key on page 194.

13. In Other Words   Look at the of Road Test Score Sheet below. With a partner, try to understand why Dennis failed his driving test. Then use idioms from the box to state what Dennis did wrong.

ROAD TEST SCORE SHEET

Name of Applicant: **Dennis Otis** _____   Date of Birth: **2/14/72**

Examiner: **David Wong** _____   Test Date: **2/17/00**

- -

A. Beginning of Test/Leaving Curb
     1. Doesn't look 10
     2. Doesn't use signal . . . .（5）
     3. Uses mirrors only . . . .（5）

B. Attention while Driving
     4. Doesn't yield to pedestrians . .（15）
     5. Reacts slowly to dangers 10
     6. Doesn't notice signs for
        railroad or driveway ahead . . . 10

C. Use of Lanes
     7. Excessive use of left lane 10
     8. Doesn't signal when
        changing lanes 10
     9. Doesn't look when
        changing lanes 10

D. Speed while driving
    10. Drives too fast . . . .（10）
    11. Drives too slowly 10
    12. Doesn't adjust speed
        as needed 15

E. Turns (including U-Turns)
    13. Doesn't signal 10
    14. Turns wide or cuts corners . . .（5）
    15. Doesn't stop and wait when
        turning left . . . .（10）
    16. Excessive speed in turn . . . . .（10）
    17. Can't make 3-point turn 15

F. Going in Reverse and Parking
    18. Doesn't signal . . . .（5）
    19. Doesn't use caution . . . .（10）
    20. Needs too much space or
        parks too far from curb 5

G. Control of Automobile
    21. Doesn't yield to pedestrians . . 15
    22. Reacts slowly to dangers 10
    23. Doesn't notice signs for
        railroad or driveway ahead . . . 10

TOTAL POINTS: __**75**__

- -

Applicant Approved for License: [ ] yes   [✔] no

If No, Reason(s) for Failure:
      [✔] more than 30 points above   [ ] accident during the test
      [ ] not enough experience with the vehicle   [ ] dangerous action

back up	*make a right/left*	*pull out*	*run over*	*start out*
keep on going	*pull into*	*pull up*	*slow down*	*turn around*

14. Describe the Cartoon   Look at the cartoon. With a partner, write sentences about what's happening in each picture. Use as many idioms as you can from the box below the cartoon. Then read your descriptions to the class.

back up	*fill up*	*pull into*
end up	*head for*	*watch out*

1. _____

   _____

   _____

2. _____

   _____

   _____

3. _____

   _____

   _____

4. _____

   _____

   _____

15. Review the Idioms   With a partner, decide which of the activities below will help you learn the most.

- Write the meaning of each idiom.

- Write a sample sentence for each idiom.

- Give examples of subjects and/or objects that go with each idiom. (Note: Not all idioms require objects.)

  EXAMPLE: <u>This class</u> has almost wrapped up <u>this chapter</u>.
             S   O

- Practice saying the idioms with correct stress. (Verbs and adverbs/particles are stressed, but the verbs *to be* and *to have* and one-syllable prepositions are not stressed.) If possible, practice saying the idioms in sentences.

Then use the list that follows to help you complete the activities together. Note the two symbols for objects.

> ( ) = The object of the preposition. It goes after the preposition.
>
> [ ] = The object of the phrasal verb. If it is a pronoun, it goes between the verb and adverb/particle. If it is a noun, it can go between the verb and the adverb/particle *or* after the adverb/particle.

1. back up; back [ ] up _____

    _____

2. block [ ] off _____

    _____

    Usage: Often passive voice: *Chestnut Street was blocked off.*

3. end up; end up in ( ) _____

    _____

4. fill [ ] up _____

    _____

5. head for ( ) _____

    _____

6. keep on going _____

    _____

    Usage: Often shortened to *keep going*

7. make a right/left; take a right/left _____

_____

8. make good time _____

_____

9. pull in; pull into ( ) _____

_____

10. pull out; pull out of ( ) _____

_____

11. pull over; pull [ ] over _____

_____

12. pull up; pull [ ] up _____

_____

13. run [ ] over _____

_____

14. slow down _____

_____

15. start out; start out in ( ) _____

_____

16. turn around; turn [ ] around _____

_____

17. watch out; watch out for ( ) _____

_____

Usage: Usually imperative: *Watch out!*

Chapter 9 — FASHION

GETTING STARTED

1. Game: Bingo   The object of the game is to fill a row of the Bingo board with names of different classmates. Go around the room and ask your classmates yes/no questions based on the board, for example, "Do you wear jeans a lot?" If the answer is yes, write that student's name in the square. If the answer is no, ask another question or go to a different student. When you have completed a row—horizontally (—), vertically (|), or diagonally (\ or /)—say "Bingo!" The first student to say "Bingo" wins and reads all the completed sentences to the class.

Samvel				
wears jeans a lot.	wears clothes for only 1 season.	makes his or her own clothes.	buys clothes from catalogs.	wears only sports clothes.
	Yuko	_Samuel_		
shops for clothes on the Internet.	buys fashion magazines.	loves to shop for clothes.	hates to shop for clothes.	wears the same clothes every day.
Sume		**F R E E**		_Samvel_
spends a lot of money on clothes.	doesn't think about fashion.		wears hand-me-downs[1].	wears different clothes every day.
		Yuko	_Vanesa_	_Samvel_
wears clothes for 10 years or more.	buys clothes in thrift shops[2].	wears Levi's jeans.	doesn't like to wear jeans.	buys clothes made in other countries.
	Yuko	_Sume_		
knows what's fashionable.	can name 5 fashion designers.	thinks clothes should be tight.	thinks clothes should be loose.	buys only clothes made in his or her country.

[1] *hand-me-downs*: used clothes from an older sister or brother
[2] *thrift shops*: stores that sell used clothing

INTRODUCTION OF IDIOMS

2. Read Between the Lines   Read the television feature story. With a partner, try to understand what it means. Then do Exercise 3.

Coming Up with a Gold Mine

What is blue, has two legs, comes in all shapes and sizes, and can be found walking on every continent? If you haven't guessed, the answer is blue jeans. When did blue jeans first **come out** and how did they get so popular?

In 1849, gold was discovered in the California hills, and one hundred thousand people streamed into the state to find gold and get rich.[3] A few years later, in 1853, a Jewish immigrant from Bavaria[4] named Levi Strauss opened a textile business in San Francisco. Strauss and his partner Jacob Davis **came up with** a smart idea in 1873: They would make tough pants for California's workers—the gold miners, farmers, cowboys, and the growing number of factory workers.

They **put together** a durable fabric and copper rivets to produce pants that wouldn't **wear out**. Their product was so original that they got a government patent for their rugged work pants. Originally, they called them "Levi's waist overalls," but in time they were called just "Levi's."

In the 1870s, Levi's were used mainly for work. But a hundred years later, they had become associated with play, rebellion, rock 'n' roll, and especially youth. Blue jeans became the uniform of the baby boomers—Americans born between 1945 and 1963—and even presidents started **rolling up** their sleeves and **showing up in** jeans. By the time the boomers had their own children, the average teenager in the United States was buying eight to twelve pairs of jeans a year.

Some teenagers were wearing baggy jeans with their shirts **hanging out**, like the rap singers they admired. Others **tucked in** their shirts and preferred pants that **fit like a glove**. These were easy to **zip up** because they were made of stretch denim. This tight-fitting style let them **show off** their slim figures.

Over the years, jeans have never really **gone out of style**, although the cut of the leg has changed with time. Today, a customer can go into a store and **try on** bootleg jeans, bellbottoms, hip-huggers, or loose-fit jeans. But pants were only the beginning for Levi Strauss & Company. Next, denim reinforced with copper rivets was **made into** shirts, jackets, and even suits, so customers could either **dress up** or **dress down** in denim.

By the end of the twentieth century, competitors such as the Gap, Tommy Hilfiger, Calvin Klein, and Polo Ralph Lauren were selling blue jeans and reducing Levi Strauss's share of the market. Lower-priced brands sold by Wal-Mart, Sears, and J.C. Penney also hurt Levi's sales. (Levi's represented 50 percent of all jeans sold in 1990, but only 25 percent in 1999.) Despite the competition and recent plant closings, Levi Strauss & Company has **grown into** the biggest brand-name clothing company in the world as well as the largest provider of blue jeans.

And so, ladies and gentlemen, while he didn't know it, Levi Strauss started his own gold rush, which has lasted more than a century after the California Gold Rush that lured him to San Francisco.

[3] called the Gold Rush
[4] *Bavaria*: part of Germany; formerly a kingdom

3. Line by Line   With a partner, mark the answer that explains the television feature story on page 126. Then look at the story and find the sentence or phrase with the same meaning. Write that sentence or phrase below. (Note: One question requires two sentences.)

1. When did Levi Strauss and Jacob Davis think of the idea of making rugged work pants for workers?

   a. [ ] In 1849
   b. [ ] In 1853
   c. [ ] In 1873

   Sentence: _____

2. How did Levi Strauss and his partner make the pants?

   a. [ ] They combined a strong fabric and copper rivets.
   b. [ ] They let workers make their own pants.
   c. [ ] They used gold to make them.

   Sentence: _____

3. What was so good about the work pants Levi Strauss made in the nineteenth century?

   a. [ ] They weren't very expensive, so everyone could buy them.
   b. [x] They remained in good condition for a long time.
   c. [ ] They fit well and looked nice.

   Sentence: _____

4. How do the children of baby boomers like to wear their shirts?

   a. [ ] They all wear their shirts outside their pants.
   b. [ ] They all wear their shirts inside their pants.
   c. [x] Some wear their shirts outside their pants, some wear them inside.

   Sentence: _____

5. Why are some tight jeans easy to close?

   a. [ ] They are made of stretch denim.
   b. [ ] They have copper rivets.
   c. [ ] They don't have zippers.

   Sentence: _____

6. What kind of jeans can be considered for purchase in stores today?

   a. [ ] Tough trousers for gold miners
   b. [ ] Only tight jeans that are made of stretch denim
   c. [ ] Bellbottoms, hip-huggers, and bootleg and loose-fit jeans

   Sentence: _____

4. Paraphrase the Magazine Article   Read the magazine article about Levi's. Work with a partner. For each idiom in bold, find the meaning in the box. Write the letter of the idiom next to its meaning.

LONG-LASTING LEVI'S

The first blue jeans (a.) **came out** in the 1870s when Levi Strauss and his partner (b.) **made** a durable fabric and copper rivets **into** rugged work pants. Originally for workers, today Levi's are worn by everybody. Since Jimmy Carter was in the White House, American presidents have (c.) **rolled up** their sleeves and (d.) **shown up in** blue jeans. Whether you like to (e.) **show off** your figure with jeans that (f.) **fit like a glove**, or you like to wear them loose, Levi's is the brand for you. And whether you need to (g.) **dress up** or (h.) **dress down**, Levi's blue jeans never (i.) **go out of style**. Levi Strauss & Co. has (j.) **grown into** one of the largest suppliers of blue jeans in the world.

____ 1. are quite tight

____ 2. appeared someplace wearing

____ 3. wear more formal clothes

____ 4. display proudly

____ 5. became available

____ 6. become over time

____ 7. shortened by folding

____ 8. start to look old-fashioned

____ 9. changed into, transformed into

____ 10. wear informal clothes

5. Figure It Out   Mark the answer that is closest in meaning to each idiom. Compare answers with a partner and try to agree.

SITUATION I: Two friends jogging in the park

1. Brenda: Somebody just **came up with** a way to make running shoes last longer.

   a. [ ] told me   b. [ ] thought about   c. [ ] invented

2. Karen: Really? When are they **coming out**?

   a. [ ] going to be available   b. [ ] going to be researched
   c. [ ] going to be seen in races

SITUATION II: A salesperson and a customer in a women's clothing store

3. Salesman: Our clothes never **go out of style**. That's why our stores are always so crowded.

   a. [ ] become fashionable   b. [ ] look old-fashioned   c. [ ] feel uncomfortable

4. Helen: Yes, you've **grown into** a very successful chain of stores.

   a. [ ] become   b. [ ] changed location   c. [ ] stayed the same

SITUATION III: Two friends getting ready for a party

5. George: If you **tuck** your shirt **in**, maybe it won't look so big.

   a. [ ] put it inside something else   b. [ ] make shorter   c. [ ] iron

6. Ted: Maybe I should just **make** it **into** a tablecloth.

   a. [ ] cover it with   b. [ ] change it into   c. [ ] wear it as if it were

SITUATION IV: Two women discussing another woman at a party

7. Cindy: Look at Linda **showing off** her figure.

   a. [ ] hiding   b. [ ] talking about loudly   c. [ ] displaying proudly

8. Doris: She *has* lost a lot of weight, but she still doesn't know how to **put** an outfit **together**.

   a. [ ] combine pieces to make   b. [ ] sew   c. [ ] go shopping for

SITUATION V: A father and son outside on a cold day

9. Father: How can you **zip up** that jacket? It's too tight.

   a. [ ] open the zipper of   b. [ ] close the zipper of   c. [ ] fix the zipper of

10. Son: No, it's fine, really. This jacket **fits like a glove**.

    a. [ ] is too loose   b. [ ] is too tight   c. [ ] is the right size

6. Choose the Right Clothes   With a partner, match each invitation with the right clothes.

a. Help us celebrate Emma's 5th birthday at a pool party

Sunday, August 2
12:00–3:00

b. The Spring Ball

Saturday, May 7th

Ballroom dancing from 8 'til midnight

Black tie

c. A 4th of July Barbecue at the Jordans.

Time: 1:00

Come as you are.

d. A cocktail party at the Waltons

Friday, June 7th

From 6 to 8

_____ 1. I need to **try on** my gown (or tuxedo), to see if it still fits.

_____ 2. I can **get dressed up** a little.

_____ 3. I can **show up in** whatever I'm wearing right now.

_____ 4. I can wear a bathing suit with a T-shirt over it. Obviously, I'm going to **dress down**.

7. Game: Same Reactions   Form teams of 4. Divide each team into 2 pairs. In pairs, discuss each situation below, decide whether or not it's OK, and check the appropriate column. Don't show your answers to the other pair on your team. When you finish, compare answers with the other pair on your team. Your team (all 4 of you) gets a point if both pairs have checked the same reaction to a situation. (A maximum of 8 points is possible.) The team with the most points wins.

SITUATIONS	REACTIONS	
	It's OK.	It's not OK.
1. Bill has decided to dress down for the holiday party at his office this year.		
2. In the middle of an important meeting, Josh told his boss that her blouse was hanging out in the back.		
3. When the air conditioner broke on a hot day, a few of the lawyers removed their jackets and ties and rolled up their sleeves.		
4. One cold day, Nina's boss wore an expensive fur coat to work. Nina asked her if she could try it on.		
5. Evan's shoes were really worn out, but they were so comfortable that he wore them to work every day.		
6. During a presentation at a sales meeting, the label on the back of Robert's jacket was showing. When Rita saw it, she tucked it in for him.		
7. Jim started dating a woman he worked with, but he didn't like the way she dressed. On the second date, he told her that her clothes had gone out of style years ago.		
8. Friday was Henry's last day of work, so he didn't get dressed up. He wore jeans.		

8. Where Do You Put "It"? Read each sentence. If the pronoun object is in the right position, mark *OK*. If the pronoun object is in the wrong position, write in the correct phrase. Compare answers with a partner and try to agree.

1. This is a great sweater for you. Why don't you try <u>it</u> on?

   OK [ ]   Correction: _____

2. All of our products are sold separately. You have to put together <u>them</u> yourself.

   OK [ ]   Correction: _____

3. Did you really wear that ridiculous costume to the party? I can't believe you showed up <u>it</u> in.

   OK [ ]   Correction: _____

4. Those shorts look a little long. You can roll <u>them</u> up, you know.

   OK [ ]   Correction: _____

5. She just renovated her apartment, and now she wants to show off <u>it</u>.

   OK [ ]   Correction: _____

6. I can see your undershirt in the back. Why don't you tuck <u>it</u> in?

   OK [ ]   Correction: _____

7. She always gives her clothes to charity before she wears out <u>them</u>.

   OK [ ]   Correction: _____

8. The zipper on this jacket must be broken. I can't zip up <u>it</u>.

   OK [ ]   Correction: _____

9. Listen and Answer   The following conversations take place in a clothing store. Listen to each conversation and the question that follows it. Read the three choices below and mark the one that answers the question correctly.

1. a. [ ] She likes the style, but her mother doesn't like it.
   b. [ ] She thinks it looks old-fashioned.
   c. [ ] She likes the style but doesn't have the money to buy it.

2. a. [ ] She asks when the new styles for the fall will be available in the store.
   b. [ ] She asks which clothes college students usually buy for school.
   c. [ ] She asks when the fashion designers will be in the store.

3. a. [ ] He's been looking for the right color pants.
   b. [ ] He's been checking pants to see if they fit.
   c. [ ] He's been getting tired of waiting.

4. a. [ ] She wants him to wear the jacket open.
   b. [ ] She wants him to buy the jacket even if it's too tight.
   c. [ ] She wants him to close the jacket to see if it's too small.

5. a. [ ] He doesn't need new running shoes.
   b. [ ] He should buy new running shoes more often, before they get too old.
   c. [ ] He should buy new running shoes when they have holes in them.

6. a. [ ] She has to adjust the length and make the sleeves shorter.
   b. [ ] She has to try the new department for short women.
   c. [ ] She has to stop eating rolls and lose some weight.

7. a. [ ] She agrees with the man.
   b. [ ] She thinks it's fashionable to combine stripes and plaids.
   c. [ ] She prefers to wear just stripes.

8. a. [ ] He shouldn't wear those clothes to the new restaurant.
   b. [ ] He can wear those clothes with the shirt outside his pants.
   c. [ ] He can wear those clothes with the shirt inside his pants.

9. a. [ ] He asks what she thinks his boss will do if he wears the pants to work.
   b. [ ] He asks if she thinks he should bring the pants to the office to show to his boss.
   c. [ ] He asks what she thinks his boss's reaction will be if he sends him a pair of the pants.

10. a. [ ] She has to wear a dress that's comfortable for dancing.
    b. [ ] She has to wear something that looks fancy.
    c. [ ] She can wear anything she wants to the dance.

Check your answers in the Answer Key on page 196. For ones you found difficult, read the Tapescript on page 181–182.

 **SPEAK UP**

10. Let's Get Personal   Is this you? For each statement, circle *True* or *False*. In a small group, share your answers. Are the other students in your group just like you?

1. I don't like to get dressed up.   True   False

2. I always try clothes on before buying them.   True   False

3. I'd be embarrassed to wear clothes that were worn out.   True   False

4. I buy new sports equipment as soon as it comes out.   True   False

5. I would never show up for work in casual clothes.   True   False

6. People say I come up with some strange ways of dressing.   True   False

7. When my clothes go out of style, I give them to people who need them.
True   False

8. I'm not the type of person who likes to show off in front of others.   True   False

9. In the warm weather I don't tuck in my shirts.   True   False

10. I always dress down on the weekends.   True   False

▶ FOR AN EXTRA CHALLENGE: After sharing your answers, go back and circle the idiom in each sentence. Check your answers in the Answer Key on page 195.

11. Giving Advice   In a small group, discuss what the salesperson could say to help the customer in each situation. Use idioms from the box to give advice. (Note: Some idioms can be used more than once.) Write your answers below.

come out	*go out of style*	*show off*
dress up	*hang out*	*try on*
fit like a glove	*roll up*	*wear out*

1. Customer: I like to buy suits I can wear for a long time.

   Salesperson: _____Try this suit on! It will never go out of style._____

   _____

2. Customer: These boots are a little old-fashioned. I really wanted to buy the latest style.

   Salesperson: _____

   _____

3. Customer: I need a pair of shoes with strong soles. I do a lot of walking, and all my shoes have holes in them.

   Salesperson: _____

   _____

4. Customer: This shirt is great. I love the color, but the sleeves look a little long. You don't have any smaller sizes. I looked.

   Salesperson: _____

   _____

5. Customer: These pants are my size, but I bet they're too small. I don't know if I should buy them or not.

   Salesperson: _____

   _____

6. Customer: This shirt looks strange inside the pants, doesn't it?

   Salesperson: _____

   _____

7. Customer: I lost thirty pounds recently. I'm so proud of myself.

   Salesperson: _____

   _____

8. Customer: I have to attend a college graduation next weekend. I don't know what to wear.

   Salesperson: _____

   _____

9. Customer: I'd love to buy another pair of these boots. I wear them all the time, and they still look new.

   Salesperson: _____

   _____

10. Customer: Do you think these pants look good on me?

    Salesperson: _____

    _____

WRITE IT OUT

12. **Create a News Story**   Before the next class, go out on the street and observe what people are wearing. Look for people who wear their clothes with style, unusual items, and the latest trends. Take pictures if you can. Write your observations as a news story, using as many idioms as you can from the list on pages 136–138. Then read your story to the class.

EXAMPLE:

Animal Instincts

Some men in the city, tired of basic khakis and blue jeans, are **showing up in** animal prints—leopard spots, zebra stripes—when they're **dressing down**. Brightly colored fabrics **made into** casual pants are popular with younger men. Floral prints—water lilies and sunflowers—are worn with T-shirts **hanging out**. And, for the somewhat older man, pants made of madras plaids, last seen in the '60s, have **come out** once again . . . .

LOOK IT OVER

13. **Review the Idioms**   With a partner, decide which of the activities below will help you learn the most.

- Write the meaning of each idiom.

- Write a sample sentence for each idiom.

- Give examples of subjects and/or objects that go with each idiom.
  (Note: Not all idioms require objects.)

  EXAMPLE: <u>This class</u> has almost wrapped up <u>this chapter</u>.
          S   O

- Practice saying the idioms with correct stress. (Verbs and adverbs/particles are stressed, but the verbs *to be* and *to have* and one-syllable prepositions are not stressed.) If possible, practice saying the idioms in sentences.

Then use the list that follows to help you complete the activities together. Note the two symbols for objects.

> ( ) = The object of the preposition. It goes after the preposition.
>
> [ ] = The object of the phrasal verb. If it is a pronoun, it goes between the verb and adverb/particle. If it is a noun, it can go between the verb and the adverb/particle *or* after the adverb/particle.

1. come out _____

_____

2. come up with ( ) _____

_____

3. dress down _____

_____

4. dress up; dress [ ] up; get dressed up _____

_____

5. fit like a glove _____

_____

6. go out of style _____

_____

7. grow into ( ) _____

_____

8. hang out _____

Usage: Informal

9. make [ ] into ( ) _____

_____

10. put [ ] together _____

_____

11. roll [ ] up _____

_____

12. show off; show [ ] off _____

_____

13. show up; show up in ( ) _____

_____

14. try [ ] on _____

_____

15. tuck [ ] in _____

_____

16. wear out; wear [ ] out _____

_____
Usage: Often passive: *It's worn out.*

17. zip [ ] up _____

_____

GLOBAL VILLAGE TORONTO
(The Language Workshop)
180 Bloor Street West, Suite 202
Toronto, Ontario
M5S 2V6 Canada

Chapter

10
IMMIGRATION

GETTING STARTED

1. **Share Your Reactions** In small groups, discuss the following immigration statistics. Compare immigration to the United States with immigration to your country. Share your reactions with the class.

IMMIGRANTS AND IMMIGRATION

Around the World

- A United Nations report estimated that there were 100 million immigrants worldwide at the end of the twentieth century. Such immigration represents a mass movement of people around the world.

In the United States

- During the Great Migration, 1880–1930, 23 million immigrants, mostly Europeans, arrived.

- There were more than 24 million immigrants as of 1996, almost 10 percent of the population. About 915,900 new immigrants arrived that year.

- Near the end of the twentieth century, about two-thirds of immigrants had completed high school.

- About 95 percent of Asians and more than 91 percent of Hispanics were living in urban areas (cities) in 1996.

Sources: The United Nations; The U.S. Bureau of the Census; The U.S. Immigration and Naturalization Service

INTRODUCTION OF IDIOMS

2. Read Between the Lines   Read the presentation a student gave to her American history class. With a partner, try to understand what it means. Then do Exercise 3.

Putting Down Roots, Then and Now

Immigration to the United States at the beginning and end of the twentieth century shows many similarities, but some significant differences, too. In fact, recent trends suggest that a new form of immigration is evolving.

From 1901 to 1910, 8.8 million immigrants arrived in the United States. In 1907 alone, a record 1.3 million people **packed up** their belongings and **set out for** a new home. They left their homelands, for the most part in southern and eastern Europe, to escape poverty, land shortages and crowding, political troubles, and religious persecution. When they arrived, they discovered, however, that they had to work long and hard just to **scrape by**. While many had come expecting to find jobs, **put away** some money, and then return home, in fact, only about a third did **go back to** the old country. Most stayed to start a new life and **put down roots** in their new land.

Not all of the newcomers were from Europe, however. Between 1901 and 1910, young men from Japan came to work as agricultural laborers and railroad hands in the West. In addition, political upheaval and economic hardship in Mexico **drove** many Mexicans **out of** their country at the start of the Mexican Revolution in 1911. Seeking freedom from political repression, and looking for economic opportunity, they also labored on the farms, for the railroads, and in the mines in the West.

Concerned that numbers beyond what the country could absorb were flowing in, the U.S. Congress decided it was necessary to **clamp down on** immigration by 1921. Congress set a ceiling of 357,000 immigrants per year and established quotas[1] for European countries. In 1924, the total to be admitted was lowered to 164,000 per year, and country quotas, especially for southern and eastern Europe, were reduced further.

After World War II (1939–1945), Congress vacillated over immigration policy. On the one hand, Japanese and other non-Caucasian immigrants who previously did not **have the right to** become citizens, could now apply for citizenship. On the other hand, for the first time, quotas were imposed for Asian countries. Responding to criticism, by 1965 Congress instituted sweeping changes, such as **doing away with** the country quotas. However, lawmakers also limited the total number of immigrants to 290,000, with preference given to the professionals and highly skilled applicants the country needed.

---

[1] *quotas*: limits on numbers

These changes in immigration coincided with political and economic changes in Asian and Latin American countries. More Asian immigrants, especially Chinese and Filipinos, began to arrive. The flow of Hispanic immigrants also increased, with Mexicans by far the largest group. By 1990, 83 percent of all new immigrants **came from** Latin America and Asia, rather than Europe.

As the end of the century drew near, the number of immigrants continued to rise rapidly. During the 1980s, a total of 8 million people—2 million of these were undocumented—entered the United States, for an average of 800,000 a year. In 1990 and 1991, the old 1907 record of 1.3 million was surpassed, although more than half were undocumented workers permitted to stay because of a special amnesty program. For all the fine-tuning in policy, the number of immigrants arriving at the end of the century was close to that at the beginning of the century.

Why do people continue to immigrate to the United States these days? The reasons are similar to those in the past: They wish to escape poverty, unemployment, growing populations, political instability, and religious or ethnic persecution. Many who come are **taking advantage of** a new policy of family reunification, which lets relatives join family members already here.

While the numbers and reasons for coming have not changed much, the destinations have changed a bit. Early in the century, immigrants represented more than 60 percent of the population of industrial cities such as Chicago, Pittsburgh, Philadelphia, and New York. Travel was difficult and expensive then, and the jobs were in the cities, so most immigrants had limited choices. In addition to the availability of jobs, many immigrants **opted for** the cities because it was easier to **blend in**. There, they found communities of their fellow countrymen who spoke their language and helped them obtain work.

More recently, however, the cheaper cost of travel and availability of jobs across the country has enabled immigrants to settle in all regions of the United States. No longer do the older, eastern cities host most newcomers. Today, many immigrants **wind up** living **in** Los Angeles, San Diego, Houston, Phoenix, and elsewhere. At the end of the twentieth century, almost 60 percent of the population of Miami, Florida was born abroad.

Finally, the contact immigrants have with their homeland has vastly changed. At the beginning of the century, once they arrived here, most immigrants were **cut off from** their homeland and their loved ones. Their only means of communication was the painfully slow mail. Today, in contrast, modern air travel and telecommunications allow immigrants to travel home and communicate frequently with family members. Now, some immigrants actually divide the year between two countries, a new phenomenon called transnationalism. With these developments, the traditional concept of immigration may be changing forever.

3. **Line by Line**   With a partner, mark the answer that explains the presentation on immigration on pages 140–141. Then look at the presentation and find the sentence or phrase with the same meaning. Write that sentence or phrase below. (Note: One question requires two sentences.)

1. How many people put their personal possessions in suitcases and left home to come to the United States in 1907?

   a. [ ] About 9 million people
   b. [ ] About 23 million people
   c. [ ] About 1.3 million people

   Sentence: _____

2. What did immigrants at the beginning of the century discover when they arrived in the United States?

   a. [ ] They had to work hard for many hours just to be able to manage with very little.
   b. [ ] They were expecting to find work but couldn't find any.
   c. [ ] There were land shortages and crowding, political trouble, and other problems in the United States, too.

   Sentence: _____

3. What did many immigrants at the beginning of the century plan to do?

   a. [ ] Stay in their new country forever
   b. [ ] Work, save money, and go home
   c. [ ] Find their relatives and live with them

   Sentence: _____

4. What percentage of immigrants at the beginning of the century returned to their homeland?

   a. [ ] About one-third
   b. [ ] About two-thirds
   c. [ ] About half

   Sentence: _____

5. What did most immigrants at the beginning of the century actually do?

   a. [ ] They returned home after making a lot of money in the United States.
   b. [ ] They called home often and reported on their progress in the United States.
   c. [ ] They began a new life and made the United States their new home.

   Sentence: _____

6. In the 1920s, how did Congress react to the number of immigrants coming into the country at the beginning of the twentieth century?

   a. [ ] Congress didn't react at all.

   b. [ ] Congress allowed more immigrants into the country.

   c. [ ] Congress allowed fewer immigrants into the country.

   Sentence: _____

7. After World War II, was there a change in the treatment of Japanese immigrants?

   a. [ ] Yes, they were given permission to apply for citizenship.

   b. [ ] Yes, they were no longer permitted to apply for citizenship.

   c. [ ] No, there was no change in their treatment.

   Sentence: _____

8. By 1965, what did Congress do about country quotas?

   a. [ ] Congress kept the quotas the same.

   b. [ ] Congress established new quotas.

   c. [ ] Congress ended the quotas.

   Sentence: _____

9. At the end of the twentieth century, what helped some people who wanted to come to the United States?

   a. [ ] They used a new policy that allowed them to escape poverty.

   b. [ ] They used a new policy that allowed them to escape religious persecution.

   c. [ ] They used a new policy that allowed them to join family members in the United States.

   Sentence: _____

10. Why did immigrants at the beginning of the century choose to live in the cities?

   a. [ ] They had lived in cities at home and had worked in factories there.

   b. [ ] That's where the jobs were and they could mix easily with people who spoke their language.

   c. [ ] Their families lived there and they could live with family members.

   Sentence: _____

4. Paraphrase the Questions and Answer Them

Part 1

List A and List B both contain questions about immigration in the twentieth century. The questions in List A use idioms from the presentation on pages 140-141. The questions in List B paraphrase them. With a partner, match each question from List A with a similar question from List B.

List A

____ 1. How many **set out for** the United States?

____ 2. Where did they **come from**?

____ 3. What **drove** them **out of** their homeland?

____ 4. Where did they **wind up**?

____ 5. To what extent were they **cut off from** their homeland?

List B

a. What was their homeland?

b. Where did they finally live?

c. How many left home to come to the United States?

d. How isolated were they from home?

e. What forced them to leave home?

Part 2

Look at the questions in List A above and write short answers for the time periods indicated.

Immigration to the United States in the Twentieth Century	
Beginning of the Century	**End of the Century**
1. _____	1. _____
2. _____	2. _____
3. _____	3. _____
4. _____	4. _____
5. _____	5. _____

5. Figure It Out Mark the answer that is closest in meaning to each idiom. Compare answers with a partner and try to agree.

SITUATION I: Two friends discussing one's new boyfriend

1. Chris: I really like Eduardo, but I'm afraid he wants to **go back to** Buenos Aires someday.

    a. [ ] leave   b. [ ] return to   c. [ ] visit

2. Marsha: Well, you could **wind up in** Argentina with him. I think that would be exciting.

    a. [ ] visit   b. [ ] move to right now   c. [ ] live in someday

SITUATION II: Two managers discussing immigration issues at their company

3. Ms. Dixon: Our company got in trouble when the Immigration and Naturalization Service started to **clamp down on** illegal aliens and require employers to check the documents of new employees.

    a. [ ] become more relaxed about   b. [ ] become stricter with   c. [ ] look for

4. Mr. Paley: I heard. Our boss didn't think the I.N.S. **had the right to** force employers to check documents.

    a. [ ] could legally   b. [ ] wanted to   c. [ ] should

SITUATION III: Two friends discussing a third friend

5. Wendy: Well, it certainly looks as if your friend Jin An Shi has **put down roots**.

    a. [ ] planted a garden   b. [ ] settled in one place   c. [ ] earned a lot of money

6. Tze: Yes, last year she was just **scraping by** and thinking about returning home, but this year she's buying an apartment and starting a family.

    a. [ ] managing with little money   b. [ ] earning lots of money
    c. [ ] looking for a job

SITUATION IV: Two students discussing exams

7. Hannah: I wish the university would **do away with** exams. They really don't tell you what students know.

    a. [ ] change the policy of   b. [ ] end the policy of   c. [ ] ask our opinion about

8. Georgina: I would **opt for** a pass-fail system if I had a choice.

    a. [ ] choose   b. [ ] end the policy of   c. [ ] make changes to

SITUATION V: Two employees going to their bank on payday

9. Hillary: You must have a lot of money in the bank. You **put away** every penny you earn.

    a. [ ] save   b. [ ] use   c. [ ] donate

10. Ryan: As soon as I have enough money, I'm **setting out for** Australia.

    a. [ ] dreaming about   b. [ ] getting a job in   c. [ ] going to

6. Fill In the Missing Idioms Read the letter to the editor of a local newspaper. With a partner, fill in each blank with an idiom from the box that follows. Then discuss your reaction to the letter.

To the Editor,

In a recent article, "The Melting Pot² Isn't Melting Anymore," the writer complains that immigrants are no longer (1.) _____ with the majority of the population. Well, how can they? Most recent immigrants, who (2.) _____ Latin America and Asia, live in urban areas. But non-Hispanic whites have (3.) _____ and left the cities to move to the suburbs. They say they were (4.) _____ by high crime rates, rising rents, and deteriorating public schools. They want to (5.) _____ the safer neighborhoods and better schools outside the cities. Since 85 percent of African-Americans still live in metropolitan areas, this leaves only immigrants and blacks (currently the largest minority) in the cities. How can the immigrants "melt" if they are (6.) _____ the majority? Perhaps if more whites stayed in urban areas instead of (7.) _____ what's called "white flight," our society would be more of a melting pot today.

Shirley Gao
Los Angeles, Jan. 5th

blending in	*driven out*	*packed up*
come from	*opting for*	*take advantage of*
cut off from		

---

² *melting pot*: a place where there is a mixture of people of different nationalities and races

7. Where Do You Put "It"? Read each sentence. If the pronoun object is in the right position, mark *OK*. If the pronoun object is in the wrong position, write in the correct phrase. Compare answers with a partner and try to agree.

1. The airlines have just lowered the cost of flying to Latin America. You should take advantage <u>it</u> of.

   OK [ ]   Correction: _____

2. The leaders of the ethnic group that drove out <u>them</u> last year will be held responsible.

   OK [ ]   Correction: _____

3. He loved money and put <u>it</u> away as fast as he could.

   OK [ ]   Correction: _____

4. The ex-president was *forced* into exile. He didn't opt <u>it</u> for.

   OK [ ]   Correction: _____

5. Countries in the European Community have ended checks at the border. It's great to see these countries doing away with <u>them</u>.

   OK [ ]   Correction: _____

6. They're glad to be home with their friends and family. They hated being cut off from <u>them</u>.

   OK [ ]   Correction: _____

LISTEN IN

8. Listen and Paraphrase   The following messages were recorded on telephone answering machines. Listen to each message. Read the three choices below and mark the one with almost the same meaning.

1. a. [ ] The man wants to know Linda better.
   b. [ ] The man is upset about what he and Linda discussed last night, but he doesn't think she is upset.
   c. [ ] The man wants to discuss their problems. He doesn't want to be alone in the end.

2. a. [ ] Jeff lives with his family but doesn't want to.
   b. [ ] Jeff does not live with his family and feels isolated.
   c. [ ] Jeff has fought with family members, but is going to visit them.

3. a. [ ] Barbara took all her things and went somewhere.
   b. [ ] Barbara's husband left her and doesn't want to talk about it.
   c. [ ] Barbara wants to see her husband today or tomorrow.

4. a. [ ] Regina loves the man who is calling.
   b. [ ] The man is surprised that Regina wants to return to her ex-husband.
   c. [ ] The man has no idea what Regina wants to do or who she loves.

5. a. [ ] The woman thinks Charles never tells her how he feels about her.
   b. [ ] The woman thinks Charles said the right thing in front of their friends.
   c. [ ] The woman thinks Charles can say how he feels, but not in front of their friends.

6. a. [ ] The parents hope their daughter can be strong and survive this difficult time.
   b. [ ] The parents think their daughter is too strong to accept help from them.
   c. [ ] The parents want their daughter to accept money from them instead of struggling by herself.

7. a. [ ] The problem is that Hannah doesn't like expensive restaurants.
   b. [ ] The man says he's sorry he wasn't free to go to the restaurant with Hannah last night.
   c. [ ] The man didn't want to spend money because he's saving for a house.

8. a. [ ] The woman wants to be an engineer, but the man hates the idea.
   b. [ ] The woman doesn't get along with the man's friends.
   c. [ ] The man hates engineers.

9. a. [ ] The man just returned from a camping trip this morning.
   b. [ ] The man is camping now.
   c. [ ] The man is going on a camping trip in the morning.

10. a. [ ] Stacey wants to have a dress code at work.
    b. [ ] Stacey wants to end the dress code at work.
    c. [ ] Right now, employees can wear whatever they want at work.

Check your answers in the Answer Key on page 197. For ones you found difficult, read the Tapescript on page 182.

SPEAK UP

9. Let's Get Personal   Is this you? For each statement, circle *True* or *False*. Share your answers in a small group. Are the other students in your group just like you?

1. When I'm setting out on a trip, I always have a lot to do at the last minute.
   True   False

2. Nothing could drive me out of my homeland.   True   False

3. I usually opt for the easiest solution to a problem.   True   False

4. I don't think immigrants should have to go back to their country if they don't want to.   True   False

5. I haven't really taken advantage of what my parents have offered.   True   False

6. I will probably wind up living in a different country from the one I'm in now.
   True   False

7. I never learned how to put money away for the future.   True   False

8. I'm the type of person who can scrape by in a difficult situation.   True   False

9. When I travel, people usually know where I come from.   True   False

10. Wherever I go, it's easy for me to blend in.   True   False

 **FOR AN EXTRA CHALLENGE:** After sharing your answers, go back and circle the idiom in each sentence. Check your answers in the Answer Key on page 197.

10. Debate an Issue

Read the following statements and choose the one you agree with:

> *For* open immigration: People should have the right to live in any country they wish.

> *Against* open immigration: Countries have the right to clamp down on the number of immigrants they admit.

Find other classmates who chose the same statement. In a small group, prepare arguments and specific examples to support your statement. Use as many idioms from the chapter as possible. One student should take notes. Choose a student from your group to debate a student from a group with the opposite point of view. Choose a moderator for the debate. The moderator should set a time limit and manage the debate.

11. Spell It Out   Choose a. or b. below.

a.   Think about an immigration experience: your own, a friend's, a relative's, or another person's. Write what happened when that person left home and immigrated to the new country. Use as many idioms as you can from the list on pages 151–152. Then read your story to a small group. Answer any questions the students have. Revise your story.

b.   With a partner, look at the pictures of immigrants below, and choose the picture that interests both of you. Together, write a story to go with the picture. Use as many idioms as you can from the list on pages 151–152. Then read your story to a small group. Answer any questions the students have. Revise your story.

12. Review the Idioms   With a partner, decide which of the activities below will help you learn the most.

- Write the meaning of each idiom.

- Write a sample sentence for each idiom.

- Give examples of subjects and/or objects that go with each idiom.
  (Note: Not all idioms require objects.)

  EXAMPLE: This class has almost wrapped up this chapter.
                    S   O

- Practice saying the idioms with correct stress. (Verbs and adverbs/particles are stressed, but the verbs *to be* and *to have* and one-syllable prepositions are not stressed.) If possible, practice saying the idioms in sentences.

Then use the list that follows to help you complete the activities together. Note the two symbols for objects.

( ) = The object of the preposition. It goes after the preposition.

[ ] = The object of the phrasal verb. If it is a pronoun, it goes between the verb and adverb/particle. If it is a noun, it can go between the verb and the adverb/particle *or* after the adverb/particle.

1. blend in; blend in with ( ) _____

_____

2. clamp down on ( ) _____

_____

3. come from ( ) _____

_____

4. cut off from ( ) _____

_____

Usage: Often passive voice: *They were cut off from their family.*

5. do away with ( ) _____

_____

6. drive [ ] out; drive [ ] out of ( ) _____

_____

7. go back; go back to ( ) _____

_____

8. have the right to ( ) _____

_____

9. opt for ( ) _____

_____

10. pack up _____

_____

11. put [ ] away _____

_____
Usage: With this meaning, the object is usually money.

12. put down roots; put roots down _____

_____

13. scrape by _____

_____
Usage: Informal

14. set out; set out for ( ); set out on ( ) _____

_____

15. take advantage of ( ) _____

_____

16. wind up; wind up in ( ) _____

_____
Usage: Often followed by a gerund: She wound up staying in Chicago.

CHAPTERS 6–10

1. Contrasting Idioms   Underline the idiom that correctly completes each sentence. Then compare answers with a partner and try to agree.

Elena always wanted to drive across the United States, so the first thing she did when she arrived in this country was buy a used car. A few days later, she was going to [1. set aside / set out for] the West Coast. She didn't want to [2. put down roots / put up with] in California; she just wanted to see the beaches, the giant Redwood trees, Hollywood, and Disney World. When she told her parents about her plan, they didn't [3. back up / back her up]. They [4. got out of / got hung up on] the fact that she was going to drive all that way alone. They [5. had nothing against / had the right to] her desire to see the country. They were just worried that something might happen to her on the way.

Before Elena left, her parents told her a lot of stories about things that had happened to young women driving alone. They gave her a lot of advice. They told her not to [6. make eye contact / make good time] with any strangers. They said when she [7. pulled into / pulled over] a gas station, she shouldn't tell anyone where she [8. came out / came from] or where she was going. And if someone tried to talk with her when she got out of her car to stretch her legs, she should just [9. go back to / go out of style] her car and [10. pull up / pull out of] the gas station. They wanted to [11. make a right / make the point] that a friendly stranger could actually be a robber or murderer.

After a while, all the stories and advice started to [12. take advantage of / take their toll on] Elena. She began to [13. come out / come to terms with] all the dangers of driving across the country alone. Soon she [14. came up with / came from] a new plan: She would borrow travel videos from the library and see the country from home.

2. The Right Response

Part 1

Read each line of a conversation between two employees at the same company. Fatima is telling Martin what she is going to say at the staff meeting the next day. Martin doesn't say much; he mostly paraphrases what Fatima says and gives support. With a partner, write the letter of each of Martin's responses next to Fatima's lines.

FATIMA

_____ 1. At our staff meeting tomorrow, I hope you'll **back** me **up** when I mention the problems we've been having with our computers.

_____ 2. I guess we'd better **point out** the problems we're having with the office staff, too.

_____ 3. I hope I don't **end up** getting fired.

_____ 4. I think we **have the right to** ask for assistance when we need it.

_____ 5. Well, it'll be interesting to see how this **plays out**.

MARTIN

a. We were told when we were hired that our supervisors must help if we ask for it.

b. Don't worry. I'll support everything you say.

c. Yeah, I can't wait to see what develops.

d. Don't worry. In the end, you're not going to lose your job for being honest.

e. Yes, it would be good to highlight them as well.

Part 2

Read each line of a conversation between a husband and wife. Angelica discusses her husband's behavior the previous night. Pedro responds to, clarifies, or paraphrases what Angelica says. With a partner, write the letter of each of Pedro's responses next to Angelica's lines.

ANGELICA

_____ 1. I don't know why you **blew up** last night at dinner.

_____ 2. Well, you seemed so angry. It took you an hour to **calm down**.

_____ 3. I'm glad you haven't **lost sight of** the good things in our relationship.

_____ 4. Well, let's not let that happen again. These little fights **take their toll**.

_____ 5. I guess we should try not to **get on each other's nerves**.

PEDRO

a. Well, I was finally able to relax when I realized that we do still love each other.

b. I think they bother you more than they bother me.

c. Stop exaggerating. I was just a little annoyed. I didn't explode, or anything.

d. Yes, let's not bother each other. Let's just be quiet.

e. Oh, no. I've very aware of what we have together.

3. It's News to Me   Read each example of authentic language taken from newspapers and magazines and try to notice the idioms. With a partner, discuss the meaning of each idiom in that particular context. Write the idiom and its meaning below.

1. From an article in *People* magazine about the actress and movie producer Goldie Hawn. It examines why she's still so popular after so many years in Hollywood.

> Hawn, 53, says that over the years she herself has pondered the sense of identification that audiences seem to feel and that the best explanation she can come up with is a simple one: "I live through my heart. Maybe that's what it is."

_____ = _____

2. From an article in *The New York Times* about autism, a developmental disability that affects the way a person communicates with and relates to people.

> The New Jersey story is not over yet, but it points toward the usual ending: the mystery of autism remains unsolved.
> Since the disorder was identified in 1943, researchers have tried to pin down its origins. Some explanations were prompted as much by cultural assumptions as by science.

_____ = _____

3. From an essay in *The New York Times* on NATO's involvement in Kosovo. The author mentions Woodrow Wilson, who was president of the United States from 1913 to 1921.

> Wilson was an arrogant idealist, a troublemaking rearranger of national borders who summed up his vision thus: "Every people has a right to choose the sovereignty under which they shall live." (Great principle; bad sentence structure.)

_____ = _____

_____ = _____

4. From an article in *The New York Times* about NATO's bombing of the former Yugoslavia.

> For the time being, the air campaign is likely to obscure the tougher questions about the future. But sooner or later they will have to be confronted, and the longer the discussion is postponed, the likelier it is that NATO's intervention in Kosovo will wind up being a failure, despite the honorable motives of those who see no alternative but to undertake it.

_____ = _____

5. From an article in *The New York Times* about clothing donations in a time of prosperity.

> Providence, R.I.—Hour by hour, cars and trucks back up to the Salvation Army's warehouse loading dock on the edge of the prosperous East Side here and disgorge clothing. . . . Beyond clearing their closets, donors have a monetary incentive for giving away clothes here. They can claim a tax deduction if they ask for a form when they pull in.

_____ = _____

_____ = _____

4. What Would *You* Say? Work in small groups. Read each situation. What would you say? Use one or more of the idioms in the box to respond to the situation. One student begins. The next student continues until all the responses build into a story, perhaps even a strange one.

1. At the company you work for, you've noticed that one employee in your department seems uncomfortable.

   EXAMPLE RESPONSES

   Student A: I've noticed that you **feel out of place** in our department. I thought maybe we should talk about it.

   Student B: You know, you **have the right to** move to a different department if you can't **put up with** the people in this department.

blend in	get on (one's nerves)
cope with	have the right to
end up	make eye contact
feel out of place	pin down
get hung up on	put up with

2. A close friend spent a lot of money on a new suit for work but then discovered that he or she didn't need to get dressed up for the job. When your friend tried to return the suit, the salesperson said they didn't give money back; instead, they gave store credit. But your friend needed the money to buy casual clothes at another store, since that store sold only suits and formal wear.

calm down	point out
dress up	put up with
go back	show up in
make a point	try on
opt for	wind up

3. The person you're dating is having problems with his or her parents, and now it's hurting your relationship. You've been fighting a lot.

ask for trouble	*have nothing against*
be fed up with	*head for*
come to terms with	*lose sight of*
cope with	*play out*
cut it out	*wrangle over*

5. **Game: Charades**   In a small group, each student silently chooses one (or more) of the idioms in the box and acts it out for the rest of the group. The others in the group must guess which idiom is being acted out.

draw one's attention to	*fill up*
be fed up with	*make eye contact*
calm down	*roll up*
dress down	*show off*
feel out of place	*try on*

CHAPTERS 1–10

1. Noticing and Understanding Idioms in a Song   Read the lyrics for the song "Take It Easy," recorded by The Eagles, and circle any idioms from this book. Compare answers with a partner, and discuss the meaning of the idioms in the context of the song.

Take It Easy[1]

Well I'm a-runnin' down the road

try'n to loosen my load,

I've got seven women on my mind.

Four that wanna own me,

two that wanna stone me,

one says she's a friend of mine.

Take it easy, take it easy.

Don't let the sound of your own wheels

drive you crazy.

Lighten up while you still can,

don't even try to understand,

just find a place to make your stand,

and take it easy.

Well I'm a-standin' on a corner in Winslow, Arizona

and such a fine sight to see.

It's a girl, my Lord, in a flatbed Ford,

slowin' down to take a look at me.

---

[1] Words and music by Jackson Browne and Glenn Frey, recorded by The Eagles. Courtesy of Warner Bros. Publications.

Come on, baby, don't say maybe,

I gotta know if your sweet love

is gonna save me.

We may lose, and we may win,

but we will never be here again,

so open up, I'm climbin' in,

so take it easy.

Well I'm a-runnin' down the road

try'n to loosen my load,

got a world of trouble on my mind.

Lookin' for a lover

who won't blow my cover,

she's so—hard to find.

Take it easy, take it easy.

Don't let the sound of your own wheels

drive you crazy.

Come on, baby, don't say maybe,

I gotta know if your sweet love

is gonna save me.

Oh, we got it easy.

We oughta take it easy.

2. Noticing and Understanding Idioms in Conversation   Read the conversation. It contains idioms from several chapters. With a partner, underline the idioms and try to understand their meaning in this context. Then discuss whether or not you agree with Carole and Bob.

Today, Carole and Bob receive their children's report cards from high school. Later that night, they discuss their children's performance. They agree that their kids, Ashley and Matt, started out well, but have been slowing down and showing less and less interest in their classes.

Carole: Frankly, I was shocked when I saw their grades. I think it's something we have to come to terms with right away. They seem to have lost interest in learning.

Bob: I agree. I think we have to make the point that it's not OK.

Carole: I've asked both of them about it, but it's impossible to pin them down. Ashley won't make eye contact with me. Matt just says "Lighten up, Mom." Then, if I try to continue, he gets fed up and won't talk it over at all.

Bob: I know one culprit is television. It's really gotten out of hand. They watch far too much.

Carole: I saw a bumper sticker today that said: "Trash your TV before it trashes you." I laughed. Then I cried when I thought of all the bad shows I've watched over the years. I don't want our kids to live like that, Bob.

Bob: There *are* some good shows, but, you're right, a lot of them are a waste of time.

Carole: If we bring this up with the kids, however, we'll wind up wrangling over it for hours.

Bob: Do we want to cut it out entirely? You and I like to watch television, too.

Carole: The problem is we let them get away with watching hour upon hour!

Bob: So what are we going to do? Tell them it's only for us? We'd be asking for trouble. They'd drive us crazy.

Carole: You're right. Maybe we can limit it to shows we're really fond of, like "Nature," "The News Hour," tennis, and . . .

Bob: Hold on. You see? We're asking for trouble. The only way is to cut it out entirely.

Carole: Trash it, then?

Bob: Recycle it . . . I don't know . . . maybe somebody can make it into a computer monitor.

Carole: Great idea! That's why I'm crazy about you. Shall we do away with it while the kids are at school or shall we come up with some way to get it out of the house as a family?

Bob: How about a farewell party? We'll celebrate. We'll sing: "So long, it's been good to know you, so long . . ."

Carole: Then we'll have time to talk, read . . .

Bob: And other things . . .

Appendix A
LIST OF PREPOSITIONS AND PARTICLES

A *particle* is an adverb that combines with a verb to form a new unit of meaning. Particles, like most verbs, are assigned stress, for example: hold ón, move ín.

A *preposition* is a word that has a tendency to occur with certain verbs. Often the meaning of the combination is not very different from the meaning of the verb alone. A preposition requires an object. One-syllable prepositions are unstressed, for example: cope with it (*cope* is stressed, but *with* is unstressed); bet on it (*bet* is stressed, but *on* is unstressed). Two-syllable prepositions are stressed, for example: move ínto it, wrangle óver it.

Prepositions	Particles/Adverbs
about	about
across	across
against	—
—	ahead
along	along
around	around
—	aside
at	—
—	away
—	back
behind	behind
by	by
down	down
for	—
from	—
in	in
into	—
like	like
of	—
off	off
on	on
onto	—
out	out
over	over
to	to
—	together
up	up
with	—

Appendix B

IDIOMS LISTED ACCORDING TO PREPOSITIONS AND PARTICLES

about
be crazy about

across
come across as

against
have nothing/something against

ahead
go ahead, go ahead with

along
get along, get along with

around
fool around, fool around with
get around, get around town
turn around

aside
set aside

at
be at a loss for words
be driving at

away
do away with
get away with
put away

back
go back, go back to

behind
be behind bars

by
scrape by

down
boil down to
calm down

clamp down on
dress down
gun down
pin down
put down roots, put roots down
slow down
track down

for
ask for trouble
be at a loss for words
fall for
head for
make room for
opt for
set out for
spell out for
watch out for

from
come from
cut off from

in
blend in, blend in with
break in
cash in on
coop up in
do in
eat in
end up in
fall in love, fall in love with
hide out in
lock up in
move in
pull in
show up in
start out in
tuck in
wind up in

into

break into
build up into
grow into
make into
move into
pull into
run into
talk into

like

fit like a glove

of

be/become fond of
bow out of
drive out of
feel out of place
get out of
get out of hand
go out of style
kick out of
lose sight of
move out of
pull out of
take advantage of

off

block off
cut off (*interrupt*)
cut off from (*separate from*)
make off with
pay off
show off
take off
take one's mind off
throw off

on

be/go on the market
be on the run
be on the wrong track
bet on
cash in on
clamp down on
come on
get hung up on
get on one's nerves
hold on

keep an eye on
keep on going
look out on
put on
put the blame on
set out on
take its toll on
try on

onto

hold onto

out

bow out, bow out of
branch out
buy out
clean out
come out
cut it out
dish out
drive out, drive out of
eat out
feel out of place
get out, get out of
get out of hand
go out of style
hang out
hide out in
kick out, kick out of
look out on
move out, move out of
play out
point out, point out to
pull out, pull out of
put out
set out, set out for
ship out
spell out, spell out for
start out, start out in
turn out
watch out, watch out for
wear out
work out

over

blow up over
bowl over
hand over
have over

pull over
run over
start over
talk over, talk over with
wrangle over

to
boil down to
come to terms with
draw attention to
go back to
go to trial
have the right to
own up to
point out to

together
put together

up
back up (*support*)
back up (*go in reverse*)
beat up
be fed up, be fed up with
blow up, blow up over
break up
bring up, bring up with
build up, build up into
come up with
coop up, coop up in
dress up, get dressed up
end up, end up in
fill up
fix up
get hung up on
keep up
lighten up
lock up, lock up in
make up
own up to
pack up
pass up
pick up
pull up
put up with
roll up
set up

show up, show up in
stay up
sum up
tie up
wind up, wind up in
wrap up
zip up

with
be fed up with
blend in with
bring up with
come to terms with
come up with
cope with
do away with
do business with
fall in love with
fool around with
get along with
get away with
go ahead with
hold one's own with
make eye contact with
make off with
put up with
talk over with
wreak havoc with

Miscellaneous Idioms
(without prepositions or particles)
change course
do time
drive crazy, drive mad
keep a stiff upper lip
keep going
make a right/left, take a right/left
make eye contact
make good time
make money
make a point, make the point
shift gears
surf the Net
take it easy
take its toll
take one's pick

Appendix C
IDIOMS LISTED ALPHABETICALLY

Idiom	Chapter	Idiom	Chapter
ask for trouble	7	cut it out	7
back up (*support*)	6	dish out	7
back up (*go in reverse*)	8	do away with	10
be at a loss for words	1	do business with	2
beat up	7	do in	5
be behind bars	4	do time	4
be crazy about	5	draw attention to	6
be driving at	1	dress down	9
be fed up, be fed up with	7	dress up, get dressed up	9
be fond of, become fond of	5	drive crazy, drive mad	5
be on the market, go on the market	2	drive out, drive out of	10
be on the run	4	eat in	3
be on the wrong track	6	eat out	3
bet on	2	end up, end up in	8
blend in, blend in with	10	fall for	5
block off	8	fall in love, fall in love with	5
blow up, blow up over	7	feel out of place	7
boil down to	6	fill up	8
bowl over	5	fit like a glove	9
bow out, bow out of	2	fix up	3
branch out	2	fool around, fool around with	5
break in, break into	4	get along, get along with	1
break up	7	get around, get around town	3
bring up, bring up with	1	get away with	4
build up, build up into	2	get hung up on	6
buy out	2	get on one's nerves	7
calm down	7	get out, get out of	7
cash in on	2	get out of hand	4
change course	2	go ahead, go ahead with	1
clamp down on	10	go back, go back to	10
clean out	3	go out of style	9
come across as	5	go to trial	4
come from	10	grow into	9
come on	1	gun down	4
come out	9	hand over	7
come to terms with	6	hang out	9
come up with	9	have nothing/something against	6
coop up, coop up in	3	have over	3
cope with	7	have the right to	10
cut off (*interrupt*)	1	head for	8
cut off from (*separate from*)	10	hide out in	4

165

Idiom	Chapter	Idiom	Chapter
hold on	1	put up with	7
hold one's own with	5	roll up	9
hold onto	3	run into	5
keep an eye on	5	run over	8
keep a stiff upper lip	5	scrape by	10
keep on going	8	set aside	6
keep up	3	set out, set out for, set out on	10
kick out, kick out of	7	set up	2
lighten up	1	shift gears	5
lock up, lock up in	4	ship out	2
look out on	3	show off	9
lose sight of	6	show up, show up in	9
make a point, make the point that	6	slow down	8
make a right/left, take a right/left	8	spell out, spell out for	1
make eye contact, have eye contact	7	start out, start out in	8
make good time	8	start over	1
make into	9	stay up	3
make money	2	sum up	6
make off with	4	surf the Net	2
make room for	3	take advantage of	10
make up	2	take it easy	1
move in, move into	3	take its toll, take its toll on	7
move out, move out of	3	take off	2
opt for	10	take one's mind off	7
own up to	4	take one's pick	3
pack up	10	talk into	1
pass up	3	talk over, talk over with	1
pay off	2	throw off	1
pick up	4	tie up	4
pin down	6	track down	4
play out	6	try on	9
point out, point out to	6	tuck in	9
pull in, pull into	8	turn around	8
pull out, pull out of	8	turn out	5
pull over	8	watch out, watch out for	8
pull up	8	wear out	9
put away	10	wind up, wind up in	10
put down roots, put roots down	10	work out	2
put on	1	wrangle over	6
put out	2	wrap up	1
put the blame on	4	wreak havoc with	6
put together	9	zip up	9

Appendix D
STUDENT B'S DIRECTIONS FOR
INFORMATION GAP EXERCISES

Chapter 4 Crime

11. Information Gap: Communicate and Collaborate

Student B's Directions, Part 1

You are a law professor and crime expert. Student A is a news reporter preparing an article on famous crimes of the twentieth century. Student A will ask you questions about the O. J. Simpson case. Read about the case below and use the information to answer Student A's questions.

When you are finished, go to Part 2 on page 168. Now *you* will ask questions about another famous crime.

The O. J. Simpson Murder Trial

O. J. (Orenthal James) Simpson was a famous football player and sports announcer. He was married to Nicole Brown Simpson. She was the mother of two of his children. The couple divorced, however, after a stormy marriage.

On the night of the murders in 1994, Nicole Simpson's mother had forgotten her glasses at a restaurant. Later that night, Ronald Goldman, a waiter at the restaurant and also a friend, brought the glasses to Ms. Simpson's home. Outside the house, the two were stabbed to death with a knife.

The police questioned O. J. Simpson about the murders and decided to arrest him. But Mr. Simpson left home with a close friend in the friend's car. The police chased the car. The chase was videotaped and shown on television. Mr. Simpson was eventually locked up and remained in jail until the case went to trial.

The case was talked about and written about a lot because Mr. Simpson was rich, famous, and popular. The case also interested people because Mr. Simpson was African-American, and Ms. Simpson and Mr. Goldman were white.

The criminal case went to trial in September, 1994, and was televised. Mr. Simpson's lawyers presented two theories about the crime. First, the lawyers said that a close female friend of Nicole Simpson was a drug user, so it was probably some drug dealers who killed Ms. Simpson and Mr. Goldman. Second, the lawyers said that Mark Fuhrman, one of the police officers at the scene of the crime, was a racist and wanted people to think that Mr. Simpson was the murderer. The lawyers believed he tried to make Mr. Simpson look responsible for the crimes by planting evidence at Mr. Simpson's home.

The prosecutors[1] used the evidence at the Simpson house to build a case against Mr. Simpson. They said that a bloody glove and other evidence linked Mr. Simpson to the murders.

In October, 1995, the jury in the criminal case decided that the evidence did *not* prove that Mr. Simpson murdered his ex-wife and her friend. However, in a second trial—a civil suit[2]—a different jury found that Mr. Simpson *was* responsible for the deaths. Mr. Simpson did not have to go to jail, but he had to pay compensation to the families.[3]

Mr. Simpson never owned up to the murders, and the police never arrested anyone else for the killings.

Student B's Directions, Part 2

You are a news reporter preparing an article on famous crimes of the twentieth century. One of these crimes was the assassination (murder) of President John F. Kennedy in 1963.

What do you need to know about this case to write your article? The following questions will get you started:

> Was the president **gunned down** or killed in another way?
> Where and when did this happen?
> Was the assassin (the killer) **tracked down**?
> Did the case **go to trial**? If so, what happened?

Now, prepare additional questions with these idioms:

lock up	*own up to*
be behind bars	*put the blame on*

Finally, ask Student A your questions and take notes on the answers. When you are finished, go to Create a News Story on page 58 and write your article about the assassination of President Kennedy.

---

[1] *prosecutor*: government lawyer who acts for the state in a criminal case

[2] *civil suit*: a dispute between two private people that is settled before a judge or jury; penalties involve money, not jail sentences

[3] The jury awarded $8.5 million in compensatory damages to the Goldman family, and $12.5 million in punitive damages to the Goldman family and the Brown family.

7. Information Gap: Soap Opera Game   The two charts below represent the characters and events in Episode 1 and Episode 6 of a soap opera.[4] Answer your partner's questions until he or she has filled in all the blanks in his or her charts. Then ask your partner questions until you have filled in all the blanks in your charts. Do not show your charts to your partner. Try to be the first pair in your class to finish.

EXAMPLE QUESTION: Who is Eduardo Estrada **crazy about**?

Student B's Chart—Episode 1

Christina Carlucci	is married to _____.	is fooling around with Dr. Cotton.
Eduardo Estrada	is married to Christina, but thinks she's fooling around with someone he knows.	is crazy about _____.
Mrs. Kimberly Pearson	comes across as a _____ person.	wants Casilda to marry Jonathan.
Casilda Pearson	falls for Dr. Cotton.	wants to do _____ in.
Jonathan Waters	drives _____ crazy.	runs into his ex-girlfriend Jessica.
Jessica Trumbull	is still crazy about Jonathan.	meets with _____.
Private Investigator Brandon Johnson	is hired by Eduardo to keep an eye on Christina.	is bowled over by _____.
Dr. Nicholas Cotton	comes across as _____.	turns out to be a womanizer.[5]

---

[4] *soap opera*: a television serial drama series based on personal relationships and romance
[5] *womanizer*: a man who constantly chases women

Christina Carlucci	divorces _____.	runs into Jonathan and falls in love with him while having dinner with Dr. Cotton.
Eduardo Estrada	divorces Christina.	discovers that Casilda has fallen for _____ and tries to do himself in.
Mrs. Kimberly Pearson	bowls Dr. Cotton over with the news that Casilda is adopted and can't inherit her millions.	fell for _____ years ago.
Casilda Pearson	finds that _____ has changed and she is no longer crazy about him.	decides she wants to fool around with Jonathan.
Jonathan Waters	shifts gears and decides he doesn't want to be involved with any more women.	drives _____ and _____ crazy.
Jessica Trumbull	kept a stiff upper lip while _____ was fooling around.	tries to do Jonathan in when she realizes he doesn't want to be with her anymore.
Private Investigator Brandon Johnson	comes across as _____.	proposes to Christina.
Dr. Nicholas Cotton	has been keeping an eye on _____ for his partner.	hopes that Casilda will fall in love with the son of his rich partner.

▶ **FOR AN EXTRA CHALLENGE:** With your partner, write a summary of the two episodes. Use the details on the charts and add some details of your own. Share your summary with the class.

7. Information Gap: Role Play

Student B's Directions, Part 1

Read the description of the scene below. Then, read Luke's lines silently. (Do not show these lines to your partner.) After you hear Anita's first line, decide which one of Luke's lines comes next and read it out loud to your partner. Your partner will then look for the line in his or her script that goes next. Continue back and forth until you've used all your lines. Finally, put the lines in order by writing the number of the line (1–4) next to each one.

Description of the Scene

In a television studio, a soap opera is being taped. Two actors playing the roles of Anita and Luke are doing a scene. Luke is holding an envelope and staring at the ceiling. Anita is standing in front of him, looking angry. She wants Luke to give her the envelope. Anita speaks first.

Luke's Lines

____ e. Oh, quit squawking, Anita. I'm **getting out of** here. I've had enough. Goodbye.

____ f. (*Staring at the ceiling*) **Cut it out**, Anita. You're not getting it. Let's just talk.

____ g. I told you before, you're not getting that letter . . . even if you threaten to **kick** me **out of** the house again.

____ h. Why do I have to look at you? Just **calm down**.

Student B's Directions, Part 2

Read the description of the scene below. Then read the father's lines silently. (Do not show these lines to your partner.) Decide which one comes first and read it out loud to your partner. Your partner will then look for the line in his or her script that goes next. Continue back and forth until you've used all your lines. Then, put the lines in order by writing the number of the line (1–5) next to each one. Finally, choose one of the scenes (Part 1 or Part 2) and perform it in front of the class.

Description of the Scene

Shelley, age 17, has just come home from a night out. She is putting her coat away in the front hall when her father comes down the stairs, dressed in his bathrobe and slippers. Her father speaks first.

Father's Lines

____ a. No, you're **getting on** *my* **nerves**! I'm not **putting up with** this any longer.

____ b. Do you know what time it is? You're **asking for trouble**, young lady.

_____ c. Don't give me that "**calm down**" business or you'll find yourself grounded[6] for a month. Now give me the keys.

_____ d. I'm doing this for your own safety. Maybe someday you'll understand. Now go to bed.

_____ e. (*Coming over to her*) Well, I**'m fed up with** your behavior. You completely disregard my instructions. I told you I want you home by midnight. I'm going to ask you to **hand over** the car keys.

---

[6] *grounded*: a punishment in the form of losing permission to go out

Tapescript

Chapter 1 Conversational Styles

11. Listen and Paraphrase

1. A: I apologize for **cutting** you **off** again. Please, finish what you were going to say.

   B: I can't remember what it was. It probably wasn't very important.

2. A: Gee, you've told me one horror story after another. Why don't you **lighten up** a little?

   B: That's easy for you to say. You weren't personally involved in all those situations.

3. A: I'm sorry I can't help with the party preparations. Everybody's been asking me to help them with one thing or another. It's just too much.

   B: OK, **take it easy**. Sorry I asked.

4. A: You know, if we don't **wrap up** our first draft by tonight, we're not going to be able to complete our project by next week.

   B: Well, we're almost there.

5. A: Everything's easy for you. You don't have any money problems. You don't have to work like the rest of us.

   B: Hey, I don't know what you**'re driving at**.

12. Listen and Answer

1. A: I studied hard for the test, but the first essay question really **threw** me **off**. After that, I was so nervous that I couldn't answer the other questions either.

   B: I don't understand why. All the questions were discussed in the review session.

   Narrator: What did the student say about the test?

2. A: According to the computer, you have several books overdue right now, so you won't be able to borrow any more books until those are returned. As soon as you return them and pay the fine, you'll be allowed to borrow more books.

   B: Are you **putting** me **on**, or what?

   Narrator: What is the man's reaction to what the librarian said?

3. A: I know you want us to do our history projects with a partner, but my partner and I just don't **get along**. Would it be possible to do the project alone or work with a different person? I don't know what else to do.

   B: It's really too late to change partners at this point, and I *do* want you to work with somebody. You'll have to find a way to work together.

   Narrator: Why doesn't the student want to work with her partner?

4. A: Don't take that Psychology course with Professor Greenwood. Half the class failed last semester. You have too many hard courses this semester. You need something easy. How about The History of Art? The instructor is really great, and it's an easy *A*.

   B: OK, you **talked** me **into** it.

   Narrator: What did the man decide to do?

5. A: I think your topic—Social Classes in Sitcoms—is too broad. I suggest you limit it to one social class—say, the working class. You could show an increase in TV programs about the working class and explain why this is so. You should probably **start over** and bring me a new outline.

   B: Yes, but I wanted to compare the different classes in my paper.

   Narrator: What does the instructor want the student to do with his paper?

Chapter 2 Business

10. Listen and Answer

1. A: So, how did you become interested in sunglasses?

   B: I owned this lens shop—you know—for eyeglasses, and I noticed that lots of customers asked about sunglasses—good sunglasses, fashionable sunglasses—so I decided to **change course** and **cash in on** the demand for sunglasses.

   Narrator: Why did the woman start making and selling sunglasses?

2. A: Let's see . . . the company is five years old. Has your investment **paid off**?

   B: Yes. The company **took off** as soon as we started selling our first collection of sunglasses. My investment definitely **paid off**.

   Narrator: What did the woman say about the company's financial situation?

3. A: And are you thinking about **branching out**, or are you going to continue to sell just sunglasses?

   B: We're going to continue to **put out** sunglasses. That's all we want to do.

   Narrator: What did the interviewer ask the woman?

4. A: Companies need to change, don't they? What will you do in the next few years?

   B: We have a simple plan: to **build up** our selection of sunglasses.

   Narrator: What is the company's plan?

5. A: Do you **do business with** companies outside the United States as well as those inside the country?

   B: Yes, of course . . . Latin America and Japan **make up** thirty percent of our business.

   Narrator: What does the woman say about the companies that buy her sunglasses?

11. Listen, Take Notes, and Answer

Another self-made millionaire—I should say multimillionaire—is Robert Bertuglia, Jr. He was raised in a working-class neighborhood on Long Island, New York. He says he was a typical teenager: His main interests were toys, cars, and girls. He wasn't a very good student and barely graduated from high school. But what he loved, above all else, was work.

His first job was cutting grass. His mother drove him—and his lawn mower—to his jobs. Once he started **making money** by mowing lawns, he saved $250 and bought an old pickup truck for transportation. When he was still in high school, he hired his first employees and **branched out** into landscaping. While doing lawns and landscaping, he noticed that one company—a large real-estate developer—owned many of the buildings in his area. He decided to offer his landscaping services to this company. The managers laughed at the possibility of **doing business with** a high-school kid, but gave him one location, just for fun. When they saw his work, however, they weren't laughing. They offered him landscaping jobs at their other locations. Soon, they asked if he could do cleaning, too. After mowing lawns all day and supervising his eight employees, Bertuglia cleaned the company's headquarters at night.

After his first cleaning job, Bertuglia **changed course** and never looked back. Timing is everything, as they say. He **built up** his cleaning business in the 1980s when companies were replacing the better-paid union workers with non-union workers, who made just over minimum wage. Bertuglia **cashed in on** this trend. By the late 1990s, the company he **set up**, Laro Service Systems, had really **taken off**. It had become one of the largest, private building-service companies in New York, with 1,800 workers and $50 million in revenue. But for nearly two decades, Robert Bertuglia worked seven days a week, fifty-two weeks a year. Of course, this left little time for his wife and three children. Like many self-made millionaires, Bertuglia wrecked his marriage and lost his dream house in the divorce.

Chapter 3 Residence

9. Listen and Answer

Commercial 1. Are you **cooped up** in a tiny apartment with no view? Have you dreamed of living in a high-rise apartment that **looks out on** the whole city? Do you want an apartment you don't need to **fix up**? The brokers at Abigail Realty are ready to help. Call us today or visit our site on the Internet: www.abigail.com.

Commercial 2. If you're not happy with your present home, stop **holding onto** it. It's the right time to sell, and the folks at Suburban Realty are ready to help you. Whether you want to buy a small house so you don't have a lot of work to do, or a large house so you can **have** lots of friends **over**, we've got the house for you. Come in and **take** your **pick**. Call Suburban Realty today.

Commercial 3. If you're having trouble **getting around** and also need help with meals, you should consider **moving into** 30-30, a new residence for those who are sixty and over. Our staff will do all the chores you're tired of, including **keeping up** the grounds. For meals, we'll deliver a tray of food to your room or you can join friends in our beautiful dining room. Act now. Call 1-800-555-3030.

Commercial 4. Are you thinking of having a family? Do you need to **make room for** children? Would you like to **eat in** more? Apartment Dreams has lots of spacious two- and three-bedroom units with eat-in kitchens. For a limited time, we're offering free decorating services with the purchase of your apartment. Don't **pass** this opportunity **up**. Make your dreams come true. Call Apartment Dreams today.

Chapter 4 Crime

10. Listen and Answer

1. A: Why don't you tell me exactly what happened?

   B: Well, Officer, I came home from work at 6:00, but then I went to the supermarket to buy some food. I got home from the store around 6:45 and found that someone had **broken in**. My apartment door was unlocked and someone had **made off with** my TV and VCR.

   Narrator: What happened at the woman's apartment?

2. A: Did you see what happened?

   B: Yes, Officer. I was across the street the whole time. A man came out of a building with a brown paper bag in his hand. Another man came running out of the building with a gun in his hand. He **gunned down** the man with the paper bag and then **hid out** on the rooftop.

   Narrator: What did the witness see the man with the gun do?

3. A: If the case **goes to trial**, will I have to appear in court as a witness to the murder?

   B: I'm sure you'll be called as a witness, but first we have to **track down** the murderer. That's not going to be an easy job.

   Narrator: What do the police need to do now?

4. A: We need to send a car over to the university right away. The drinking **got out of hand** at a party at one of the clubs. When two students left the party, they got hit by a car and were sent to the hospital. The driver **put the blame on** the students, but the club **put the blame on** the driver.

   B: I heard that the students just walked into the street without looking.

   Narrator: What was the cause of the accident?

5. A: Officer, are you saying the person who robbed me at gunpoint has been **picked up** for the same crime before? So why **wasn**'t he **behind bars** instead of out on the street?

   B: According to our computer records, he had **done time** for robbery but was released from jail early for good behavior.

   Narrator: What did the police officer tell the woman about the robber?

6. A: Two boys **tied** my son **up**, then left him in a football field all night. If they **get away with** this, we're going to leave the state and move to a safer place.

   B: Your son will need to identify the boys who did this.

   Narrator: What will cause the woman and her family to move to another state?

7. A: The bank robbers have **been on the run** for three weeks now. We think they're **hiding out in** Philadelphia at this point.

   B: They robbed a bank in New York. Next they were seen in New Jersey. One of them has relatives in Philadelphia, so they may have gone there.

   Narrator: What have the bank robbers been doing for three weeks?

8. A: They're going to have to **lock** you **up** for now. Listen, if you **own up to** kidnapping your son from your ex-husband's house and explain to the judge *why* you did it, you might not have to spend more time in jail.

   B: But he's *my* son. Why should I say I kidnapped him? And why should I spend *any* time in jail?

   Narrator: What does the lawyer tell the woman?

Chapter 5 Love

9. **Listen, Take Notes, and Answer**

My next film is *Moonstruck*, starring Cher and Nicolas Cage. I'**m** really **fond of** this romantic comedy, with its delightful twists and opera-like variations on the theme of love. Indeed, it has the passion of an opera.

Cher plays Loretta Castorini, a graying widow in her late thirties, who works as a bookkeeper and thinks she has bad luck. She's dating Johnny Cammareri, a middle-aged Brooklyn boy who **comes across as** a dull, confirmed bachelor. Early in the film, Johnny unexpectedly proposes to Loretta in an Italian restaurant but immediately flies to Sicily to comfort his dying mother. The marriage, he announces, has to wait until he returns. He leaves Loretta instructions to invite his brother Ronny to the wedding. The brothers haven't talked in five years.

Loretta goes to the bakery where Ronny works to personally invite him. It **turns out** that Ronny, like Loretta, has had bad luck: Loretta lost her husband, and Ronny lost his hand, each in an accident. But Ronny blames *his* accident on Johnny. The result is bad blood between the brothers. When Loretta tries to talk to him, he starts chanting: "I have no life . . . I lost my hand. I lost my bride." Apparently his fiancée left him after the accident. This, it seems, has **driven** him **crazy**. A young woman who works at the bakery and who **keeps an eye on** Ronny says sadly, "I'm in love with this man, but . . . he could never love anybody since he lost his hand and his girl."

But spunky Loretta doesn't quit. She and Ronny go upstairs to his apartment where she cooks him a steak. "You'll eat this one bloody," she mothers him. They talk. Each tells the other the mistakes they've made.

He confesses that he has **fallen in love with** her, but she is stricken by a guilty conscience. They can never see each other again, she insists. He agrees only if Loretta will accompany him to the opera he **is** most **fond of**, *La Boheme*.

In preparation for their date, Loretta gets her hair done, buys a fancy dress, and is completely transformed. When Ronny meets her at the Metropolitan Opera House, he is **bowled over** by her beauty. They have a splendid time together until they **run into** Loretta's father and his girlfriend.

Meanwhile, Loretta's mother—who knows her husband is unfaithful to her, but can't understand why—goes out for dinner alone, **keeping a stiff upper lip**. Mrs. Castorini talks with a professor at the restaurant and asks him why men **fool around**. He suggests it's nerves; she thinks it's because they fear death. Mrs. Castorini, a housewife, realizes she can easily **hold her own** with the professor. That night the full moon works its magic—all are moonstruck.

The story reaches a climax when Johnny unexpectedly returns from Italy and comes looking for Loretta the next morning. Everyone has assembled at the Castorini household, and it **turns out** that Johnny feels he can't marry Loretta. He announces, "In time, you'll see that this is the best thing." She shouts, "In time, you'll drop dead, and I'll come to your funeral in a red dress!" The lines and characters are fresh and funny. In the tradition of comedy, the conflicts are resolved happily, and the characters, gathered around the Castorinis' kitchen table, toast "To Family!" I add my toast: "To *Moonstruck*!"

Chapter 6 Debate

10. Listen and Answer

1. During this holiday season, we'd like to take a minute to **draw** your **attention to** the homeless. Please help us help the homeless by sending a check to Homeless in America.

2. If you or someone you love is having trouble **coming to terms** with an addiction, call the Addiction Hotline: 1 800 G-E-T-H-E-L-P.

3. If you need surgery, you have a lot to think about. But your decision **boils down to** this: Which hospital has the best team of surgeons and the latest technology? The answer is the Surgery Hospital. It's your life. Choose wisely.

4. When a prospective employer asks you to **sum up** your work experience, do you know what to say, or do you simply clear your throat? Let our team of experts help you prepare for your next job interview. Call today: The Employment Experts, 555–1440.

5. If you never have time for friends or family, if you feel you're rushing from morning until night, you**'re on the wrong track**. We can help. Call Lifestyle Counselors today. Check your local phone book for our number.

11. Listen, Take Notes, and Answer

OK, let's see, your topic is Simple Living, An Alternative to Consumerism. You **make the point** that millions of people in the United States believe they **are on the wrong track**, spending too much time working to buy material possessions. They say consumerism is **wreaking havoc with** their lives. You **point out** that some of those who have become aware of this have chosen an alternate lifestyle, known as "voluntary simplicity."

OK, let me see. Do you explain what voluntary simplicity is? A little bit. You give examples of choosing clotheslines over clothes dryers and bicycles over automobiles. And you say that these choices involve products that are cheaper, quieter, easier to fix, and much safer for the environment. Let me see. You also mention Joe Dominguez, who worked on Wall Street but never **lost sight of** what he wanted in life. It wasn't getting rich, right? He realized that that wasn't making him or his co-workers happy. He developed some courses to help people stop thinking about making money and start thinking about making themselves happy. He **sums up** his ideas in his book *Your Money or Your Life*.

I don't think you have stated what voluntary simplicity **boils down to**. You need to do that and then **pin down** why it's more deeply satisfying than excessive consumption. You need to find some studies about people who have been living a simple life for a while, so you can show how it **plays out** over time. Once you've done that, you can use this paragraph, which asks your readers to **set aside** the fast-paced life they're used to, and begin enjoying family, friends, creative expression, and nature again.

I **have nothing against** mentioning the historical roots of this movement—the fact that the colonists depended on thrift and self-sufficiency—but I don't think the end is the place to do it. Perhaps it would fit better at the beginning.

Don't be discouraged. Generally, I was pleased with your essay. It's a good topic, one that really makes you think. You just need to provide more detail and change the order a little bit.

Chapter 7 Anger

9. Listen, Take Notes, and Answer

Today, we'll be talking about stress. I'd like you to think about how well you **cope with** stress in your life. I want you to imagine yourself in each situation I mention. Here we go. Does it **get on** your **nerves** when a friend or family member criticizes your driving? Do you **blow up** when you're at the checkout counter at the supermarket and the person in front of you goes to get one more grocery item and makes you wait? What about when you lose money in a soda machine—do you get angry? Do you scream? Curse? Hit the machine? Or are you the type of person who can **put up with** these annoyances and not let them bother you?

These may sound like minor issues, but researchers are studying whether angry responses to everyday annoyances have negative effects on your health. In a recent study, the researchers wanted to discover whether subjects—both men and women—who showed high levels of anger and hostility as college students were at greater risk for cardiovascular disease by the time they reached the age of forty. And, yes, they did find greater risk of disease in these subjects. The researchers concluded that anger **takes its toll** on your health. Now, let's look at another study which shows that women who **blow up** over little annoyances are **asking for trouble** in terms of their health.

10. Listen and Summarize

This is it! I can't **cope with** this situation anymore. You know it **gets on** my **nerves**, but you continue to do it anyway. You know you're **asking for trouble**, but you just won't stop. At this point, I**'m** completely **fed up**. I can't **take** my **mind off** it.

Are you listening to me? I'm talking to you. Why don't you **make eye contact with** me? Why don't you say something?

Listen, do you really think I'm going to **put up with** this forever? It's the little things like this that **break up** a marriage.

OK, I have to **calm down**. This is starting to **take its toll** on me. You just have to **cut it out**, that's all. I can **cope with** almost anything, but not this. I'm telling you for the last time, don't squeeze the toothpaste in the middle!

Chapter 8 Driving and Directions

10. Listen and Paraphrase

1. Hi, this is Kate Jenkins. I got your message. Just wanted to let you know that you shouldn't park on the street when you come to Jimmy's birthday party. Please **pull into** our driveway. See you Saturday.

2. Hi honey, it's seven thirty and I'm still at work. Boy, do I need this vacation! Could you get the car out of the parking lot and **fill** it **up** so we can leave as soon as I get home?

3. Welcome to Newark Airport. If you need to let passengers out of your car, please **pull over** briefly. Do not stop in the middle of the road, and do not leave your car unattended.

4. Thank you for shopping at the Suburban Mall. We appreciate your business. Please use caution as you **pull out of** the parking lot.

5. You have reached the Department of Motor Vehicles. If you wish to take a road test, drive your car to Elm Street and join the line. All tests **start out** there and end on Twelfth Street.

11. Listen and Answer

1. A: I think you passed Erica's house. You'd better **back up** and check the house numbers.
   B: There's a car behind me. I think I'll just go to the end of the block and **turn around**.
   Narrator: What does the man say he'll do?

2. A: Anita, **watch out**! You're going to **run over** that dog!
   B: Relax, I've never hit anything yet.
   Narrator: What is the passenger worried about?

3. A: We'd better **head for** the Morenos' party now or we'll **end up** in a lot of traffic and get there late.
   B: I don't care if we're late. It's not a sit-down dinner.
   Narrator: What does the woman suggest?

4. A: You know, if you **take a left** here and get on Route 206, we'll **make good time**.
   B: I didn't think we needed to rush. Why don't we take the scenic route?
   Narrator: Which way will get them there faster?

5. A: I have only one suggestion: **Slow down** a little more when you're parking.
   B: OK, but after I'm in the parking space, do you think I need to **pull up** a little to give the car behind me more room?
   Narrator: What does the woman ask the driving instructor?

Chapter 9 Fashion

9. Listen and Answer

1. A: Mom, there's no way I'm buying that dress. That kind of thing **went out of style** years ago. Why don't you buy it for yourself if you like it so much?

   B: Honey, it's a classic. It'll always look good.

   Narrator: Why doesn't the daughter want to buy the dress?

2. A: When are the fall fashions **coming out**? My daughter's going away to college and needs to buy some clothes for school pretty soon.

   B: In another week. But we have lots of things for college students right now.

   Narrator: What does the woman ask the salesperson?

3. A: Hey, I like these pants. Great color, and they look as if they're long enough. I think I'll **try** them **on**.

   B: Look, you've been doing this for an hour. I'm getting tired.

   Narrator: What has the man been doing in the store?

4. A: That ski jacket looks great, but it may be a little tight. Let's see how it looks when you **zip** it **up**.

   B: Uhh, I don't think I can.

   Narrator: What does the woman want the man to do?

5. A: You definitely need new running shoes. You know, you're not supposed to **wear** them **out**. If you run a lot, you should replace them regularly, before they look like this.

   B: I thought they were OK as long as they didn't have holes in them.

   Narrator: What does the salesperson tell the man?

6. A: It's not easy to get something that fits well when you're only five feet tall. I usually have to **roll up** the sleeves and have everything shortened.

   B: Have you tried our new Petite Department?

   Narrator: What does the customer say she has to do?

7. A: This designer has the strangest ideas about fashion. I would never **put** stripes and plaids **together**.

   B: Oh, I disagree. I think it's very fashionable.

   Narrator: What is the woman's reaction?

8. A: Honey, do you think I can wear this to that new restaurant?

   B: Sure. If you **tuck** the shirt **in**, you can.

   Narrator: What does the woman tell the man?

9. A: What do you think my boss will say if I **show up** for work **in** these pants?

   B: Ha! I think he'll send you home to change or fire you!

   Narrator: What does the man ask the woman?

10. A: I have to **get** all **dressed up** for a big dance at school. Can you suggest anything?

B: Is it formal or semi-formal?

Narrator: What does the customer tell the salesperson?

Chapter 10 Immigration

8. Listen and Paraphrase

1. Linda, I know you're upset about last night, but I'll be home in an hour and we can talk about it then. Honey, I don't want to **wind up** alone, and I don't think you do either.

2. Listen, Jeff, I realize you feel **cut off from** your family, but you can call them every week and go for a visit at least once a year. It's not so bad.

3. Barbara, I can't believe you just **packed up** and left last night. We've been married for five years. Let's try to talk today or tomorrow.

4. Regina, I'm shocked that you want to **go back to** your ex-husband. I had no idea you still loved him.

5. Charles, I just want to say that you **have the right to** tell me how you feel about me, but not in front of our friends.

6. Sweetheart, your dad and I got your message. We know this is a difficult time for you financially, and we hope you'll be able to **scrape by**. We know you're strong.

7. Hannah, I'm sorry I didn't want to go to an expensive restaurant last night. It's just that I'm trying to **put** some money **away** to buy a house.

8. Larry, I hate to tell you, but this relationship is not working. All your friends are engineers, and I just don't **blend in**.

9. Dolores, I'll be **setting out** on my camping trip first thing in the morning. Just wanted to say goodbye. I'll call you when I return.

10. Peggy, did you hear that Stacey is trying to **do away with** the dress code at work? Then we can wear whatever we want.

ANSWER KEY

No answers are given for exercises that are open-ended or personal.

Chapter 1 Conversational Styles

3. Line by Line

1. c Hold on.

2. b Whoa, take it easy.

3. a He seems to be at a loss for words.

4. b Lighten up.

5. a Do we have to start it all over again?

6. b You cut me off is what happened!

7. c Women basically want to get along with others.

8. a I didn't think I'd have to spell it out.

9. b I was hoping I wouldn't have to talk you into it.

10. b Well, your questions threw me off.

4. Paraphrase Mark's Monolog

1. e   2. d   3. b   4. f   5. g   6. a   7. c

5. Match It Up

1. c   2. e   3. a   4. f   5. b   6. d

6. Figure It Out

1. b   2. a   3. a   4. c   5. b   6. a   7. a   8. b   9. b   10. c

7. Choose the Right Card

1. b   2. c   3. d   4. a

8. It's News to Me

1. Lighten Up = Don't be so serious.   2. taking it easy = relaxing, enjoying life

3. go ahead = proceed   4. spell out = make clear, say exactly

9. Where Do You Put "It"?

1. OK   2. cut him off   3. putting us on   4. OK   5. OK

10. Game: Race to Finish the Idiom

1. along   2. on   3. on   4. over   5. on   6. over   7. off   8. up   9. up   10. at

11. Listen and Paraphrase

1. c   2. a   3. c   4. a   5. b

12. Listen and Answer

1. c   2. b   3. b   4. c   5. b

13. Let's Get Personal

For an Extra Challenge answers:

1. get along with   2. cuts . . . off   3. brings up   4. take it easy   5. talk . . . over

6. hold on   7. starting over   8. lighten up   9. wrap . . . up   10. talk . . . into

Chapter 2 Business

3. Line by Line

1. c   One hundred million copies of Windows have already been shipped out.

2. b   Personal computers (PCs) were not on the market yet.

3. c   Two years later, Allen bowed out of Microsoft but remains on its Board of Directors.

4. a   After introducing Microsoft Word and Microsoft Windows, the company took off.

5. a   By its tenth anniversary (in 1985), Microsoft was really cashing in on its software.

6. b   The company was making money, big money.

7. c   Soon, Microsoft was branching out into publishing, consulting, multimedia, on-line encyclopedias, and even language instruction.

8. b   While Microsoft will continue to put out software for the PC, the company changed course near the end of the twentieth century.

4. Paraphrase the E-mail Message

1. f   2. b   3. c   4. a   5. e   6. g   7. d

5. Understanding a Biographical Statement

1. b   2. e   3. c   4. a   5. d

6. Figure It Out

1. c 2. b 3. b 4. b 5. b 6. c 7. a 8. c 9. b 10. c 11. b 12. c

7. Who's Who?

1. d 2. c 3. h 4. a 5. f 6. g 7. b 8. e

9. Where Do You Put "It"?

1. build it up 2. OK 3. OK 4. shipping them out 5. worked it out

10. Listen and Answer

1. c 2. a 3. b 4. c 5. a

11. Listen, Take Notes, and Answer

1. b 2. a, c 3. c 4. b

12. Let's Get Personal

For an Extra Challenge answers:

1. pay off 2. make . . . money 3. change course 4. working out 5. set up

6. surf the Net 7. cash in on 8. puts out 9. bow out 10. are on the market

Chapter 3 Residence

3. Line by Line

1. c Instead of holding onto what they have and fixing it up, many want to buy a bigger home.

2. b "We've been cooped up in a small apartment long enough," explains Dawn.

3. a "With the economy doing well and our personal income up, we feel we can really take our pick of available houses."

4. b And buyers, hoping to live close to work and concerned that prices might go higher, are afraid to pass them up.

5. a Nancy Dworkin of Palo Alto, California, tells us, "We had always dreamed of a house looking out on the bay, but we just can't afford it."

6. b Her husband Steve Dworkin says, "We very much wanted a big kitchen so we could cook together and eat in a few nights a week, but a house like that is out of our price range."

7. a Others are actually moving out of the suburbs and returning to the cities where they can live in a tiny apartment . . .

4. Paraphrase the Arguments

1. d   2. e   3. c   4. a   5. b

5. Paraphrase the E-mail Message

1. d   2. a   3. c   4. b

6. Figure It Out

1. b   2. b   3. a   4. b   5. b   6. a   7. c   8. a   9. a   10. c

7. Fill In the Missing Words

a. His Point of View: 1. up   2. out   3. around   4. onto   5. up   6. out
7. have   8. up   9. stay

b. Her Point of View: 1. out   2. fixing   3. into   4. cooped   5. out   6. hold
7. making   8. over   9. up   10. looks   11. have   12. Take

8. Where Do You Put "It"?

1. OK   2. having them over   3. OK   4. fix it up   5. OK   6. OK   7. pass it up

9. Listen and Answer

1. c   2. a,b   3. b   4. a,b   5. b   6. b   7. a   8. b   9. b   10. a   11. c

10. Let's Get Personal

For an Extra Challenge answers:

1. get around / get around town   2. fix up   3. eat in   4. cooped up in   5. stay up
6. pass up   7. move out of   8. clean out   9. have . . . over   10. hold onto

Chapter 4 Crime

3. Line by Line

1. c Tragically and ironically, the next day, Mr. Clutter, his wife Bonnie, and two of their children, Kenyon and Nancy, were all gunned down.

2. c They tied the family up and then killed each one in cold blood.

3. b After the crime, Dick and Perry hid out in Mexico but soon returned to the United States.

4. c Agents from the Kansas Bureau of Investigation used these leads to track down the killers, who had been on the run for six weeks.

5. a At the end of December, Dick and Perry were picked up in Las Vegas, Nevada . . .

6. b Dick, however, never owned up to the killings.

7. c Instead, he put the blame on Perry.

4. Match It Up

1. c   2. e   3. d   4. g   5. b   6. h   7. a   8. f

5. Figure It Out

1. c   2. b   3. b   4. a   5. c   6. a   7. c   8. b   9. c   10. a

6. Match the Pictures and Sentences

1. c   2. b   3. a   4. d

7. Game: Do the Right Thing

Response 1: You are in big trouble now. You've killed a group of teenagers, and you're not going to **get away with** it. You're going to be **locked up**, and your case will **go to trial**. You'll probably have to **do time**. You get 0 points.

Response 2: You tried to be nice, but your actions were not effective. After you left the drug dealers, they laughed at you and continued to sell drugs. They know they can **get away with** it. But recently, a ten-year-old boy was **gunned down** in a drug-related fight. The neighborhood group has gone to your boss to complain. The group has **put the blame on** you for the boy's death. You decide to resign. You get 2 points.

Response 3: You have acted professionally. You have evidence on videotape that the group was selling drugs. This can be used when the case **goes to trial**. You have also **picked up** the drug dealers and **locked** them **up**, so the neighborhood group is very happy. They have asked your boss to give you a raise, and she has agreed to do it. You get 10 points (the highest score). Congratulations!

Response 4: This sounds like a good idea, but it hasn't worked for most of the drug dealers. They all said they wanted to go into the program and get help. They enrolled in the program, but most of them left the next day. Because it's a voluntary program, they could leave whenever they wanted. Only one stayed in the program and is getting help. The rest of the group **broke into** another abandoned building in the neighborhood and is **hiding out** there. They are still taking drugs and selling them in the neighborhood. You get 4 points.

Response 5: You are in big trouble now. The people in the neighborhood began punching and kicking the drug dealers. Soon, the situation **got out of hand**. Someone took out a gun and shot one of the teenagers. When the case **goes to trial**, you will be called in to explain your actions. The person who shot the teenagers will probably **put the blame on** you. You're not going to **get away with** it. Your boss will have to ask you to take an unpaid leave of absence until the trial is finished. You get 0 points.

Response 6: You have done something, and you have followed the law. However, the teenage drug dealers are still selling drugs in the neighborhood. Their parents are **doing time**, so they have no supervision at all. For now, they're **getting away with** their crimes. The neighborhood group says the situation is really **getting out of hand**. They want the drug dealers to be **locked up**. And they want you transferred to a different police precinct (neighborhood). You get 4 points.

8. It's News to Me

1. gun down = kill with a gun   2. are behind bars = are in prison; locked up = put in prison

3. get away with = do whatever one wants without punishment

9. Where Do You Put "It"?

1. OK   2. gunned him down   3. break into it   4. OK   5. lock them up   6. OK

10. Listen and Answer

1. b   2. a   3. c   4. a   5. c   6. a   7. c   8. b

Chapter 5 Love

3. Line by Line

1. b This next film, *Titanic*, just bowled me over.

2. c But the way Rose and Jack run into each other is romantic and touching . . . Rose decides to throw herself into the sea.

3. b She became fond of the spirited Jack . . .

4. c . . . the spirited Jack who managed to hold his own with that upper-class group.

5. a And the noble meeting of Rose and Jack which leads to their falling in love—to me that's possible.

6. b In a short time, they are crazy about each other, and their romance threatens Rose's engagement to Cal.

7. a In the beginning of the film, he keeps a stiff upper lip, which is indeed stereotypical.

8. a And then, when he discovers Jack's sketch of Rose wearing nothing but the blue diamond, it drives him crazy.

4. Match It Up

1. c   2. b   3. a   4. d   5. g   6. e   7. f

5. Choose the Right Card

1. c   2. a   3. b   4. d

6. Figure It Out

1. c   2. a   3. c   4. b   5. a   6. b   7. c   8. b   9. a   10. c

7. Information Gap: Soap Opera Game

Episode 1

Christina Carlucci	is married to <u>Eduardo</u>.	is fooling around with <u>Dr. Cotton</u>.
Eduardo Estrada	is married to Christina, but thinks she's fooling around with <u>someone he knows</u>.	is crazy about <u>Casilda</u>.
Mrs. Kimberly Pearson	comes across as a <u>controlling</u> person.	wants Casilda to marry <u>Jonathan</u>.
Casilda Pearson	falls for <u>Dr. Cotton</u>.	wants to do <u>Christina</u> in.
Jonathan Waters	drives <u>Casilda</u> crazy.	runs into <u>his ex-girlfriend Jessica</u>.
Jessica Trumbull	is still crazy about <u>Jonathan</u>.	meets with <u>Mrs. Pearson</u>.
Private Investigator Brandon Johnson	is hired by Eduardo to keep an eye on <u>Christina</u>.	is bowled over by <u>Christina</u>.
Dr. Nicholas Cotton	comes across as <u>a family man</u>.	turns out to be a <u>womanizer</u>.

Episode 6

Christina Carlucci	divorces Eduardo.	runs into Jonathan and falls in love with him while having dinner with Dr. Cotton.
Eduardo Estrada	divorces Christina.	discovers that Casilda has fallen for someone else and tries to do himself in.
Mrs. Kimberly Pearson	bowls Dr. Cotton over with the news that Casilda is adopted and can't inherit her millions.	fell for Jonathan years ago.
Casilda Pearson	finds that Dr. Cotton has changed and she is no longer crazy about him.	decides she wants to fool around with Jonathan.
Jonathan Waters	shifts gears and decides he doesn't want to be involved with any more women.	drives Christina and Casilda crazy.
Jessica Trumbull	kept a stiff upper lip while Jonathan was fooling around.	tries to do Jonathan in when she realizes he doesn't want to be with her anymore.
Private Investigator Brandon Johnson	comes across as professional.	proposes to Christina.
Dr. Nicholas Cotton	has been keeping an eye on Casilda for his partner.	hopes that Casilda will fall in love with the son of his rich partner.

8. Where Do You Put "It"?

1. bowled him over   2. OK   3. fell for her   4. ran into him   5. OK

9. Listen, Take Notes, and Answer

1. b   2. c   3. b   4. c   5. c   6. a   7. b   8. c   9. b   10. a

Review Chapters 1–5

1. Contrasting Idioms

1. get along with   2. are fond of   3. gets out of hand   4. talk them into   5. take it easy

2. The Right Response

Part 1

1. c   2. a   3. e   4. b   5. d

Part 2

1. b   2. e   3. a   4. d   5. c

3. It's News to Me

1. setting up = organizing, establishing   2. cash in on = make money from

3. spelled out = stated in detail   4. cooped up = restricted, confined in a limited space

5. bowled over = amazed by

4. Noticing Details About Phrasal Verbs

1. a, c, d   2. a, b, d   3. a, b, c   4. b, c, d   5. a, b, d   6. a, b, d

5. Find the Topic

1. residence   2. business   3. conversation   4. crime   5. love

6. Find the Idioms

1. buy out, ship out   2. come on, spell out   3. do time, track down

4. drive crazy, fall for   5. make room for, move out

Chapter 6 Debate

3. Line by Line

1. c Of course, during World War II (1939-45), these goals were set aside.

2. b Let's see if today's debate can pin down what is best for the country.

3. c Advertisers are constantly tempting them to buy things they don't need. The statistics on this back me up.

4. a Oh, let's not get hung up on advertising.

5. c Excessive materialism is something we have to come to terms with.

6. b A society that measures individual worth by the material things a person can afford is on the wrong track.

7. c Materialism is wreaking havoc with what we have traditionally valued: friendships, family ties, and fresh air.

4. Paraphrase the Arguments

1. c   2. f   3. d   4. g   5. e   6. a   7. b   8. h

5. Seeing Similarities

1. b, c   2. b, c   3. a, c

6. Figure It Out

1. a   2. b   3. a   4. b   5. a   6. b   7. a   8. c   9. b
10. a   11. c   12. b   13. c   14. b   15. b   16. b

7. Choose the Right Card

1. b   2. a   3. c   4. d

8. Fill In the Missing Words

1. out   2. against   3. make   4. up   5. down   6. of   7. aside

9. Where Do You Put "It"?

1. wrangling over it   2. sum it up   3. OK   4. set it aside
5. OK   6. back you up   7. OK

10. Listen and Answer

1. b   2. a   3. c   4. a   5. c

11. Listen, Take Notes, and Answer

1. b   2. a   3. c   4. a   5. b   6. c   7. a   8. c

12. Let's Get Personal

For an Extra Challenge answers:

1. draw attention to   2. wrangle over   3. set aside   4. is on the wrong track
5. backed . . . up   6. come to terms with   7. boils down to   8. points . . . out to
9. get hung up on   10. have nothing against

Chapter 7 Anger

3. Line by Line

1. b   For ten days, I would try to cope with another world. I would learn firsthand what it was like to be homeless in America.

2. a   Only a few men my own age made eye contact and perhaps wondered what happened to me.

3. c   After it happened to me a few times, I was pretty fed up with this treatment.

4. b   However, I had no choice but to put up with it.

5. b   Three or four police officers were constantly breaking up fights and telling the men to calm down.

6. a   It was one of the few diversions that could take my mind off my situation.

7. c Once, when I was in a coffee shop and a waiter told me to get out, I successfully appealed to the owner . . .

8. a The young man sitting there told me to cut it out.

9. a On my last night, after being kicked out of both the bus terminal and Grand Central Station, . . .

4. Paraphrase the E-mail Message

1. c 2. f 3. a 4. g 5. h 6. d 7. e 8. b

5. Fill In the Missing Idioms

1. dishing out 2. getting on each other's nerves 3. cope with 4. put up with

5. are fed up with 6. taking its toll 7. asking for trouble 8. calm down

6. Figure It Out

1. b 2. b 3. c 4. a 5. b 6. a 7. c 8. b 9. c 10. a

7. Information Gap: Role Play

Part 1
Anita's Lines: a. 3 b. 1 c. 4 d. 2

Luke's Lines: e. 4 f. 1 g. 3 h. 2

Part 2
Father's Lines: a. 3 b. 1 c. 4 d. 5 e. 2

Shelley's Lines: f. 2 g. 4 h. 1 i. 3

8. Where Do You Put "It"?

1. OK 2. hand them over 3. OK 4. OK 5. beat him up 6. OK

9. Listen, Take Notes, and Answer

1. b 2. b 3. c 4. c 5. a

11. Let's Get Personal

For an Extra Challenge answers:

1. take . . . mind off 2. make eye contact with 3. get on . . . nerves 4. blow up over

5. calm down 6. cope with 7. cut it out 8. feel out of place

9. put up with 10. kicked out of

Chapter 8 Driving and Directions

2. Read Between the Lines

1. Exxon   2. the mountains   3. the post office   4. McDonald's   5. at ABC Drugs

4. Match It Up

1. e   2. g   3. a   4. f   5. b   6. d   7. c

5. Sign Language

1. b   2. d   3. a   4. c

6. Figure It Out

1. c   2. a   3. b   4. a   5. c   6. b   7. b   8. a   9. b   10. c

8. It's News to Me

1. slowing down = being less busy than before

2. pulled over = moved to the side of the road

3. end up = finally arrive (*after completing graduate school*)

9. Where Do You Put "It"?

1. OK   2. OK   3. pull it up   4. turn it around   5. ended up in it

10. Listen and Paraphrase

1. b   2. c   3. b   4. a   5. c

11. Listen and Answer

1. b   2. b   3. b   4. b   5. a

12. Let's Get Personal

For an Extra Challenge answers:

1. blocked off   2. pull over   3. backing up   4. ended up   5. fill up   6. turn around
7. make good time   8. slow down   9. start out   10. keep on going

Chapter 9 Fashion

3. Line by Line

1. c Strauss and his partner Jacob Davis came up with a smart idea in 1873: They would make tough pants for California workers . . .

2. a They put together a durable fabric and copper rivets . . .

3. b . . . to produce pants that wouldn't wear out.

4. c Some teenagers were wearing baggy jeans with their shirts hanging out. . . . Others tucked in their shirts . . .

5. a These were easy to zip up because they were made of stretch denim.

6. c Today, a customer can go into a store and try on bootleg jeans, bellbottoms, hip-huggers, or loose-fit jeans.

4. Paraphrase the Magazine Article

1. f   2. d   3. g   4. e   5. a   6. j   7. c   8. i   9. b   10. h

5. Figure It Out

1. c   2. a   3. b   4. a   5. a   6. b   7. c   8. a   9. b   10. c

6. Choose the Right Clothes

1. b   2. d   3. c   4. a

8. Where Do You Put "It"?

1. OK   2. put them together   3. showed up in it   4. OK   5. show it off

6. OK   7. wears them out   8. zip it up

9. Listen and Answer

1. b   2. a   3. b   4. c   5. b   6. a   7. b   8. c   9. a   10. b

10. Let's Get Personal

For an Extra Challenge answers:

1. get dressed up   2. try . . . on   3. worn out   4. comes out   5. show up for

6. come up with   7. go out of style   8. show off   9. tuck in   10. dress down

Chapter 10 Immigration

3. Line by Line

1. c In 1907 alone, a record 1.3 million people packed up their belongings and set out for a new home.

2. a When they arrived, they discovered, however, that they had to work long and hard just to scrape by.

3. b While many had come expecting to find jobs, put away some money, and then return home, . . .

4. a ...in fact, only about a third did go back to the old country.

5. c Most stayed to start a new life and put down roots in their new land.

6. c Concerned that numbers beyond what the country could absorb were flowing in, the U.S. Congress decided it was necessary to clamp down on immigration by 1921.

7. a On the one hand, Japanese and other non-Caucasian immigrants who previously did not have the right to become citizens could now apply for citizenship.

8. c Responding to criticism, by 1965 Congress instituted sweeping changes, such as doing away with the country quotas.

9. c Many who come are taking advantage of a new policy of family reunification, which lets relatives join family members already here.

10. b In addition to the availability of jobs, many immigrants opted for the cities because it was easier to blend in. There, they found communities of their fellow countrymen who spoke their language and helped them obtain work.

4. Paraphrase the Questions and Answer Them

Part 1

1. c   2. a   3. e   4. b   5. d

Part 2

The Beginning of the Century: 1. 8.8 million from 1901–1910   2. mostly southern and eastern Europe   3. poverty, growing populations, political instability, and religious persecution 4. industrial cities such as Chicago, Pittsburgh, Philadelphia, and New York   5. Except for the mail, they were cut off.

The End of the Century: 1. 8 million during the 1980s   2. mostly Latin America and Asia 3. poverty, unemployment, growing populations, political instability, and religious or ethnic persecution   4. Los Angeles, San Diego, Houston, Phoenix, and Miami   5. They're not cut off. They can travel home and communicate frequently with family. Some spend half a year in each country

5. Figure It Out

1. b   2. c   3. b   4. a   5. b   6. a   7. b   8. a   9. a   10. c

6. Fill In the Missing Idioms

1. blending in   2. come from   3. packed up   4. driven out   5. take advantage of

6. cut off from   7. opting for

7. Where Do You Put "It"?

1. take advantage of it   2. drove them out   3. OK   4. opt for it   5. OK   6. OK

8. Listen and Paraphrase

1. c   2. b   3. a   4. b   5. c   6. a   7. c   8. b   9. c   10. b

9. Let's Get Personal

For an Extra Challenge answers:

1. setting out on   2. drive . . . out of   3. opt for   4. go back to   5. taken advantage of
6. wind up   7. put . . . away   8. scrape by   9. come from   10. blend in

Review Chapters 6-10

1. Contrasting Idioms

1. set out for   2. put down roots   3. back her up   4. got hung up on
5. had nothing against   6. make eye contact   7. pulled into   8. came from
9. go back to   10. pull out of   11. make the point   12. take their toll on
13. come to terms with   14. came up with

2. The Right Response

Part 1

1. b   2. e   3. d   4. a   5. c

Part 2

1. c   2. a   3. e   4. b   5. d

3. It's News to Me

1. come up with = think of, offer   2. pin down = identify specifically
3. summed up = stated the main ideas briefly; has a right to = can legally
4. wind up = in the end be   5. back up = go in reverse; pull in = drive in

Final Review Chapters 1-10

1. Noticing and Understanding Idioms in a Song

take it easy, drive . . . crazy, lighten up, slowin' down, come on

2. Noticing and Understanding Idioms in Conversation

INTRODUCTION: started out, slowing down

CAROLE: come to terms with

BOB: make the point that

CAROLE: pin . . . down, make eye contact with, Lighten up, gets fed up, talk . . . over

BOB: gotten out of hand

CAROLE: (*none*)

BOB: (*none*)

CAROLE: bring . . . up, wind up, wrangling over

BOB: cut it out

CAROLE: get away with

BOB: asking for trouble, drive . . . crazy

CAROLE: 're . . . fond of

BOB: Hold on, asking for trouble, cut it out

CAROLE: (*none*)

BOB: make it into

CAROLE: 'm crazy about, do away with, come up with, get . . . out

BOB: (*none*)

CAROLE: (*none*)

BOB: (*none*)

CREDITS

Text Credits

Art Credits

Page 1, first cartoon, © The New Yorker Collection 1999 J.P. Rini from cartoonbank.com. All Rights Reserved.; second cartoon, © The New Yorker Collection 1992 Richard Cline from cartoonbank.com. All rights reserved. **Page 14**, first cartoon, © The New Yorker Collection 1994 Mick Stevens from cartoonbank.com. All Rights Reserved.; second cartoon, © The New Yorker Collection 1994 Arnie Levin from cartoonbank.com. All Rights Reserved. **Page 18**, courtesy of Microsoft Inc. **Page 23**, photo of Madonna, Munawar Hosain/Fotos International/Archive Photos; photo of Yo Yo Ma by J. Henry Fair, courtesy of J. Henry Fair and International Creative Management. **Page 29**, courtesy of Ethan Allen Interiors Inc. **Page 44**, modern house, Pearson Education/PH College; traditional house, CORBIS/Dave G. Houser; city apartment, CORBIS/Lawrence Manning. **Page 61**, © The New Yorker Collection 1999 Frank Cotham from cartoonbank.com. All Rights Reserved. **Page 81**, Stock Boston, Inc./Peter Menzel 1985. **Page 96**, Pearson Education/PH College. **Page 150**, top left, early twentieth century immigrant woman, Library of Congress; top right, early twentieth century immigrant family, Photo Disc, Inc.; bottom left, modern immigrant couple w/certificate of citizenship, Tony Stone Images; bottom right, four generations of an Asian-American family, Tony Stone Images.

GLOBAL VILLAGE TORONTO
(The Language Workshop)
180 Bloor Street West, Suite 202
Toronto, Ontario
M5S 2V6 Canada